COMPLETE CREDIT AND COLLECTION MODEL LETTER BOOK

Harold E. Meyer
Scott A. Sievert

PRENTICE HALL
Englewood Cliffs, New Jersey 07632

Prentice-Hall International (UK) Limited, *London*
Prentice-Hall of Australia Pty. Limited, *Sydney*
Prentice-Hall Canada, Inc., *Toronto*
Prentice-Hall Hispanoamericana, S.A., *Mexico*
Prentice-Hall of India Private Limited, *New Delhi*
Prentice-Hall of Japan, Inc., *Tokyo*
Simon & Schuster Asia Pte. Ltd., *Singapore*
Editora Prentice-Hall do Brasil, Ltda., *Rio de Janeiro*

© 1990 *by*
PRENTICE-HALL, Inc.
Englewood Cliffs, NJ

"This publication is designed to provide accurate and authoritative information in regard to the subject matter covered. It is sold with the understanding that the publisher is not engaged in rendering legal, accounting or other professional service. If legal advice or other expert assistance is required, the services of a competent professional person should be sought.

...From the Declaration of Principles jointly adopted by a Committee of the American Bar Association and a Committee of Publishers and Associations."

10 9 8 7 6 5 4 3 2

Library of Congress Cataloging-in-Publication Data

Meyer, Harold E., 1920–
    Complete credit and collection model letter book / Harold E. Meyer
and Scott A. Sievert.
        p. cm.
    ISBN 0-13-156126-X
    1. Collecting of accounts—United States. 2. Commercial
correspondence—United States.   I. Sievert, Scott A. II. Title.
HG3752.7.U6M49 1990
658.8′8—dc20   90-6848
                                                                              CIP

ISBN 0-13-156126-X

PRENTICE HALL
BUSINESS & PROFESSIONAL DIVISION
A division of Simon & Schuster
Englewood Cliffs, New Jersey 07632

Printed in the United States of America

Acknowledgments

This book is more than the work of two authors. We gratefully recognize the following organizations that provided letters and other assistance:

Acme Scale Company
Alphagraphics
Arizona Bank, The
Artist's, The
Associated Air Freight, Inc., Carolyn Yaker
Broadway Southwest
Brunswick Corporation, Max McGrath
California Cartage Co., Inc., Wayne E. Schooling
Chemical Bank
Chevron U.S.A., Inc., Sellers Strough
Computer Products, Victoria Barklow
County of Alameda, California
Credit Bureau, The
Crown Zellerbach Corporation
Druggist, The, Cy Peterson
Dun & Bradstreet
East Chicago Machine Tool Corp.
East/West Network, Jackie Anderson
Emery Air Freight Corporation
Exxon Company, U.S.A.
Feed Barn, The
Gavilan Animal Hospital
Goldwaters, Phoenix
Goodyear Tire & Rubber Company, James R. Glass
IMCO Container Company
Interstate Commerce Commission
Klein Products, Inc.
LBJ Lumber, Inc.
Mervyn's
Midwest Bag Company

Mobil Oil Corporation
Morgan Hill Times
National Writers Union
O'Connor Hospital
Pacific Gas and Electric Company
Pacific Intermountain Express Co.
Prudential Insurance Company of America
Rosso's Furniture
Salvo Tool & Engineering, Bruce Bedker
San Jose Mercury News
Signode Corporation
Small Business Administration
Synder's of Hanover, Jean Ortiz
Southern Pacific Transportation Company
State Compensation Insurance Fund
True Value Hardware
United Parcel Service
Western Writers Workshop of Sun City, Arizona
Zellerbach Paper Company

Dedication

To Patricia and Linda

About the Authors

For over thirty years, *Harold E. Meyer* has worked closely with credit departments, accumulating, analyzing, and writing credit and collection letters, and verifying their effectiveness. Mr. Meyer is an industrial accountant with a lifelong passion for words and how they affect listeners and readers. He is a professional member of the National Writers Club, the Arizona Authors' Association, moderator of the Western Writer's Workshop, and author of the highly successful *Lifetime Encyclopedia of Letters*. He is also a former credit reporter for Dun & Bradstreet. He holds a degree in Business Administration from the University of Washington.

Scott A. Sievert has over twenty years of credit and collection experience. He is currently vice president and corporate credit manager of Ed Holderness Supplies, Inc., a wholesale distributor of hardware, lumber, construction, and mining supplies with ten divisions and subsidiaries throughout Arizona.

Sievert is also vice president of the Central Arizona Credit Association, the Consumer Credit Counseling Services, and is an advisor for the Arizona Institute of Credit.

He is a past board member of the National Association of Credit Managers (NACM) Education Association, past president of the NACM of Arizona, Inc., and is currently on their board of directors.

Sievert is an active member of several religious and civic organizations. He holds a degree in Business Administration from Arizona State University and teaches credit courses for the Maricopa County Community College District.

Contents

How This Book Will Help You Solve
Credit and Collection Problems

HOW THESE LETTERS CAN SOLVE OBSTINATE PROBLEMS

Personal visits may be the best method, but often you will find them time-consuming. Your unscheduled visit may be inconvenient for both you and your customer. A visit is a confrontation that requires an immediate response, and your customer may not want to answer right now. A phone call can have some of the same drawbacks.

A letter, on the other hand, can be read when there is time to absorb it, often costs less than a phone call, provides a permanent record, can express your personality well, and can communicate your thoughts exactly as you wish. We will show you how to write letters that produce these results.

We should point out at this time that letter writing is only one of the procedures in a complete collection effort. Telephone follow-up is usually helpful, and, on occasion, personal visits to clear complicated past due items are essential, especially in business-to-business situations. The collection process starts with a request for or offer of credit and proceeds as far as necessary, which can include settlement by court action. This book is limited to the writing of letters that may shorten that process.

Successive letters can be signed by employees of increasingly higher rank or company officers: first the accounts receivable supervisor, then the accountant, then on to the credit manager, office manager, controller, vice president, legal counsel, and company president, for example. The higher the rank of the signer, the stronger the impact.

HOW TO WRITE SUCCESSFUL LETTERS

Many business letter writers have doubts about how to write a proper letter. The common solution is to refer to a previous letter, especially if it was written by a supervisor. The supervisor probably had the same doubts—and the same solution. Thus old fashioned "business writing" has perpetuated itself with such phrases as *enclosed please find* and *be advised that.*

Part I of this book explains how to write credit and collection letters that accomplish their purposes of solving credit problems and collecting money. You will learn how and why letters to consumers and to other businesses should differ. A list of attention-getting opening sentences for collection letters is provided as well as a list of strong closings.

While most of the letters in this book are quoted directly from credit managers who found them successful, some have been modified to make them applicable to more than one situation. Because the reader is under no obligation to reply, all the letters have been worded with great care. You may not wish to copy any of the letters word for word, but they can easily be modified for your particular uses.

HOW TO MAKE THE BEST USE OF THIS BOOK

The change of a company name, the date, the dollar amount, the product, or a few words can turn one of these model letters into your own personal letter. You may wish to take a sentence or paragraph from one letter and additional sentences from another to create a letter you prefer to any of the models.

The letters in this book are proven standards that can be adapted to your requirements for many years. You will want to keep it within easy reach for daily use because of the variety of treatments and the complete range of topics.

COMPLETE RANGE OF TOPICS

This book contains 787 letters and covers 230 separate credit and collection categories or topics.

Credit situations are covered in Chapters 1, 3, 9, and 10. Among the seventy-four topics or categories to help you solve credit problems are these: New Accounts Invited; Welcoming New Customers; Bank Data Requested; Requesting Additional References; Credit Granted; Credit Limited; Credit Delayed; Credit Refused; Credit Canceled; NSF Checks; Thanks for Payment; Thanks for Partial Payment; Apology for Delay; Delayed Refund; Unidentified Deduction; Postdated Checks; Credit Policies Explained; Misunderstanding; Special Terms Denied; Guarantor's Notice; and Holiday Goodwill.

Collecting money is the subject of Chapters 2, 4 through 8, and 11 through 15. The categories range from a simple reminder, "Please Pay," to five examples of letters used by collection agencies. The letters make clear how to collect small bills and large obligations and how to retain the goodwill of your customer while being insistent enough to collect your money.

The 156 categories of collection letters include the following: Just a Reminder; Appeals to Self-Interest, Credit Standing, Fairness, Friendship, Cooperation, Duty, Honor, Fear, Sympathy, Justice, and Pride; New Start; Terms; Small Bills; Trust; Contract; Extended Payments; Patience; Reputation; Good Faith; Discounts Available; Holding Orders; Late Charges; Selling to Past Due Customers; Cash in Advance; Broken Promise; Freight Bill; Charge Account; Installments; Delinquency Report; Future Credit Limited; and Final Demand Notice.

HOW THIS BOOK IS ORGANIZED

Part I consists of two chapters revealing the best techniques available for writing effective letters relating to credit problems and for writing collection letters that accomplish the purpose of collecting your money.

Part II covers credit and collection situations involving you and your customer. Collection letters are presented in four stages: reminders, request reminders, appeals or discussions, and final demands. The final letters precede your turning the collection job over to an outside agency or attorney.

Part III presents letters written by one business person to another business person. These include more specific data than is required in letters to consumers, such as purchase order numbers, invoice numbers and shipping dates.

One special feature of this model letter book is the "How to Do It" section preceding the letters in each chapter. This item is a simple, step-by-step outline. By following the sequence, you will write well-organized letters, remember all essential parts, and eliminate unnecessary digressions.

Using the letters and suggestions in this book will enable you to collect more of the money that is rightfully yours.

Scott A. Sievert
Harold E. Meyer

Part I

HOW TO WRITE CREDIT AND COLLECTION LETTERS

CHAPTER *1*

How to Write Effective Credit Letters

Because the reputation of your firm will be reflected in the credit letters you write, they should be written to reveal the facts in a concise, polite manner. Also, because communication is between people, whenever possible you should write individual letters to particular persons rather than using a preprinted form. The word processor makes it possible to send out form letters that are individually typed or printed. Address these to the person who will make the decision you request. The decision maker can be determined by a phone call to the company. Only when this fails should a letter be addressed to a department.

REFUSING CREDIT

Many credit managers find that the most challenging letter to write is one refusing credit. The problem is how to tell a potential customer or client "No" and still leave the door open for a future business relationship. The struggling, undercapitalized business person of today may be a profitable customer a few years hence. This person may also be willing to buy on a cash basis for a while and may appreciate any cash discounts you offer. During the time this customer buys for cash, you have the opportunity to convince him or her of the benefits of using your company as a supplier; you can also tender a personal touch, so much needed in these days of hectic business dealings. Use this time to tactfully build goodwill.

How do you write a rejection letter when you wish you could simply write "No?" First, try saying "Yes" to something else. This is a buffered approach. Get your customer to relax and be comfortable. The simplest way is to thank him or her for the order or the application for credit. Be careful here not to imply that credit will be granted. For example, do not write:

> **Thank you for your order for seven washing machines. We have what we believe to be the most durable line in the industry.**

This appears to be leading to acceptance. You might write instead:

> **Thank you for your order for seven washing machines. We offer these to you this week at a discount for cash.**

Now you, as the seller, are without question implying cash rather than credit. At the same time, you are offering something to your customer but not cutting him or her off completely.

The next step is to state the reasons for your refusal of credit. Always mention the reasons before stating the refusal. It provides a logical lead into the "bad news," and by the time you have given a few reasons your reader will have come gradually to understand that a refusal is in the offing. State the reasons specifically, yet tactfully. Be clear, simple and straightforward.

The reasons may include past slowness in making payments, undercapitalization, expanding too fast, insufficient financial data, too recently employed, business not established, too much competition, and others. Don't make the reasons so short that the reader will feel offended by your curtness.

For example, you might say:

> **A close examination of your financial statements reveals that you may have difficulty meeting our terms at the present time. Your payables appear to be somewhat out of line with your receivables.**

or

> **Because your business is new and your start-up costs have been high, we feel that the credit line you have requested might put an undue burden on your ability to make payments on time.**

Now you must state the refusal. You will note that it is in the middle of a five-section letter that we couch the "bad news." It is there, but the reader has been gently led up to it and then will be gently led down to the reality that he or she must search for alternative to receiving credit from you.

An indirect refusal, the ideal kind, could be like this:

We suggest that you remain on a cash basis for the time being. Perhaps in another six or nine months you will wish to apply again.

In some instances a direct "No" will be required:

Based on the information received from many sources, we can sell to you only on a cash basis.

Even a direct refusal need not turn your customer away. Your next step is to offer your customer an alternative to credit. Some ideas:

We will be glad to reconsider your credit application in another six months.

You can take advantage of our discounts for cash.

Paying cash does not lessen our delivery or follow-up services.

If you would send us current financial statements, we would be happy to reconsider your application.

Can you provide us with the names of firms with which you have been doing business recently? We will then take another look at your credit situation.

Our quality products and rapid delivery are still available to you on a cash-with-order basis.

Just a short sentence to let your customer know that you are on his side and are willing to help in spite of his current credit problem takes the sting out of your refusal. This customer may be valuable in a few years. Look to the future.

Close your credit refusal letter with a thought that will create goodwill. A good way is to restate one of your strong selling points or to thank your reader for considering you as a supplier. For example:

Thank you for the opportunity to be of service to you.

We thank you for considering our company.

We appreciate your thinking of us as a future supplier.

Our cash customers receive the same service as credit customers do.

We carry the top two lines in the industry.

We hope we can be of further service to you in the near future.

We look forward to hearing from you in another six months.

Even a letter of refusal allows you the opportunity to show your friendly and cooperative attitude. If you have to refuse credit, try to retain the applicant as a cash customer.

Briefly, the five parts of a letter refusing credit are these:

1. Comment on some item about which you and your reader agree, or offer a thank-you.
2. Mention your reason(s) for refusing credit.
3. State the refusal.
4. Offer your customer an alternative.
5. Close with a thought that will retain your customer's goodwill.

GRANTING CREDIT

A letter granting credit is an agreeable one to write. You feel good about gaining another customer, and you are happy that you can help someone else.

While in a letter refusing credit we suggested placing the refusal statement itself in the middle of the letter to soften the impact, in a letter granting credit we suggest putting the "good news" right up front. In the first sentence you could write:

We have opened a line of credit for you (company name).

The credit you requested has been granted.

Your credit rating is excellent, and we are pleased to add you to our list of satisfied customers.

Your order No. 1477 is being shipped today. We welcome you as a new credit customer.

We are pleased to open a credit account for you.

We are happy to grant you the credit line of $2500 requested in your recent application.

Because of your excellent credit rating, we are happy to approve a charge account for you.

After a sentence or two of good news and welcome, briefly state your terms of sale. Your terms may be 1% 30 days, 2% 10 days, net 30 days, net 10 prox. or a variety of other terms. You can start the paragraph with a simple, "Our credit terms are. . . ." Then state them. Some examples:

> **Our terms are 1% 30 days net 31 days from the billing date, which is one day after the shipping date. A late charge of 1% per month is added to invoiced amounts not paid within 31 days.**
>
> **Monthly billings are due upon receipt of your bill, with a 1½% finance charge added to amounts not paid within 25 days. The ending date of this 25-day period is shown on your statement.**
>
> **Our terms are 2% 10 days net 30 days. A 1% per month finance charge is added after the 30-day period.**

In the credit-granting letter, the following topics should be omitted or mentioned only briefly: Payment options, variety of rates for financial charges, seller's rights, credit reports, and penalties for failure to pay. These can be included in a short brochure or leaflet to be enclosed with the letter, or, preferably, with your first billing.

While granting credit, you have an excellent opportunity to include a little sales pitch about what your company can do for your customer. Mention prompt delivery service, meeting shipping dates for items that must be manufactured to order, the quality of your line of goods, or other favorable factors such as these:

> **We promise next day delivery within a 100-mile radius on items in stock.**
>
> **Orders received by 10:00 A. M. can be delivered the same day.**
>
> **As a credit customer, you will receive advance notice of all sales.**
>
> **We carry nationally recognized brands.**
>
> **We sell tools of only the highest quality.**
>
> **We are never undersold. Bring us proof of a competitor's price and we will refund any difference you have paid.**
>
> **Our reputation has been built on quality and service.**
>
> **We offer complete maintenance on all products we sell.**

Close with a pleasant comment about your interest in serving your customer. For example:

We look forward to serving you.

A pleasant working relationship is anticipated.

Thank you for considering us for your needs.

Again, we welcome you as a new customer.

We are glad to have you join our growing list of satisfied customers.

Your outline for a letter granting credit can be similar to this:

1. Reveal that credit has been granted.
2. State your terms of sale.
3. Make a small sales pitch.
4. Close with a comment about your interest in serving your customer.

WELCOME

A welcoming letter to a new customer is similar to the credit-granting letter. It usually includes an explanation of the terms of sale. The differences are more emphasis on the welcoming portion and more detail about the terms. Both mention your product or service and politely encourage the customer to take advantage of your offerings.

TERMS OF SALE

There are occasions when the subject of terms of sale is the central point of your credit letter. One occasion is when your customer is making payments on a regular basis that are not in accordance with your stated terms. In this instance you would want to discuss your due dates and any discounts in detail and all the alternatives you can. You may be able to arrange terms that are close to the payment schedule apparently used by your customer.

Another occasion is when your customer has no recognizable payment schedule. In this case a discussion is necessary of what the terms mean to you and, of more importance, to your customer. You could explain that when you receive payments at a known time you can plan your receivables and thus your purchases, resulting in a more efficient, lower-cost operation. These savings can then be passed on to your customer by means of lower prices. You might mention that making prompt payments is the best way for your customer to establish and maintain a high credit rating and thus make his future purchases easier to arrange.

REQUESTING CREDIT INFORMATION

The most common letters requesting credit information from a supplier are straightforward inquiries that provide blank spaces to be filled in. This form of request is easy to answer and is more likely to elicit a response than a letter requiring an essay-type answer.

Space should also be provided for general comments by your reader. Opinions of other sellers are often as important in determining paying ability and practices as cold statistics. If you are seeking general opinions only, write a letter asking for general information that might be helpful to you in determining the credit worthiness of your customer.

State that the information you receive will be treated confidentially. When possible, mention your willingness to reciprocate by providing credit information to your reader when requested. Enclose a postpaid envelope for the convenience of your reader. This fact can be mentioned in your letter.

A wide variety of questions can be asked in your letter of inquiry. The following list includes twenty-three suggestions, but in no one letter would you want to use all of them:

Date of first sale
How long sold
Sold since
Terms
Highest credit
Highest recent credit
Your credit limit
Average credit extended
Discount period
Discounts allowed
Date of last transaction
Presently owing
Payment is prompt/slow/delinquent
Pays cash in advance

Pays C. O. D.
Takes cash discounts
Days slow
Past due
Placed for collection
Collected by attorney
Written off to expenses
Makes unjust claims
Remarks (comments)

SOLUTIONS TO OTHER CREDIT PROBLEMS

Suggested solutions to the many other credit conditions, problems, and questions that arise are offered through the letters in this book. Among these situations are: canceling credit, acknowledging orders, thanking customers for orders, extending credit limits, providing credit information, and resolving misunderstandings.

With these and other credit problems, the initial step is to reveal the purpose of your letter. Do this in the first sentence, but take care to be as polite as direct. Here are a few examples of opening sentences:

We would like to take this opportunity to welcome you as one of Compower's customers and acquaint you with our practices.

Thank you for your initial order.

Thank you for your inquiry about opening an account with Beemer, Inc.

Due to the high cost of carrying credit, we regretfully must begin charging for accounts unpaid within 30 days of service rendered.

We appreciate your explanation of your recent delay in making payments.

I am being completely honest when I say that many of our customers prefer to pay cash.

Your help in supplying the following information will be appreciated.

Enclosed with this letter is a copy of our credit policies.

With pleasure we have opened a charge account for you.

The next part of a credit letter is the clarification and expansion of your beginning statement. It is the essence of your letter, the explanation of the problem. Some examples:

> **You appear to be paying your invoices in batches rather than individually within our terms.**
>
> **We have arranged a credit limit of $5000.00 as you requested.**
>
> **I believe we've satisfactorily resolved the $737.90 balance in your account.**
>
> **We would like to open a line of credit for you, but because of the lack of information it is not possible to do so at this time.**
>
> **Your frankness in relating your recent tragedy and its effect on your business is commendable.**
>
> **We are unable to identify the invoices you are paying with this check.**
>
> **This is the third check in four months that you have sent to us unsigned.**
>
> **You still have, however, an outstanding balance of $599.50, and we know you want to clear that amount as soon as possible.**
>
> **We are making a few inquiries and will let you know the results as soon as possible.**

Having explained the purpose of your letter, what do you expect of your customer? What is he or she to do, and how? Offer a solution or suggestion. Your willingness to help solve the problem will carry over to your reader and bring forth cooperation in return. Here are some possible actions to suggest to your customers:

> **If you will mail us a current financial statement, we will be glad to review your account.**
>
> **Rather than delay the total amount due, perhaps you can make partial payments of $_____ every two weeks.**
>
> **We will be happy to extend your payment schedule if you will sign a note for a fixed amount each month, which will include both principal and interest.**
>
> **We believe that in another six months we will be able to open an account for you.**
>
> **We are willing to accept a partial payment of $40 now, and you may defer the balance until March 15.**

> **Because we cannot accept postdated checks, we must hold your order until your check clears the bank, or you can mail us a check with a current date.**
>
> **To aid us in establishing the appropriate line of credit for this account, please complete the form below and return it in the enclosed, postpaid envelope.**
>
> **Please take advantage of the 15% discount for payments made within ten days of the billing date.**

The final part of a credit letter is a request for cooperation. Each party gives a little and receives a little, making your business dealings more pleasant, a little easier, and ultimately more profitable. We offer a few ideas for your closing statement:

> **We can both benefit by your taking the 1% discount for paying within ten days.**
>
> **Thank you for this opportunity to help you with your rush order, and we hope to work with you again soon.**
>
> **We hope this extension of your payment schedule will help you recover from your fire loss.**
>
> **Thank you for your cooperation in making this change.**
>
> **An envelope is enclosed for your reply.**
>
> **Your business in a valuable asset to us and we look forward to serving your future needs.**
>
> **Our competitively priced merchandise, however, is still available to you on a cash basis.**
>
> **Your continuous promptness in making payments earns our respect.**
>
> **When your account is fully paid, we will again consider providing you with a line of credit.**
>
> **We appreciate your cooperation and hope that you will not hesitate to contact us should we ever be able to help you in a similar way.**

Our suggested steps in writing about credit situations and problems can be listed this way:

1. Reveal the purpose of your letter in the first sentence.
2. Clarify or expand your first sentence.
3. Suggest a solution to the problem or action the reader can take.
4. Ask for the reader's cooperation.

FORMAT

Every letter should include the name, mailing address, and telephone number of the writer or his company for the convenience of the reader when making a reply. To clearly identify the writer, his or her name should be typed below the signature.

SUMMARY

Credit letters vary from a simple "Thank you for your business" to a happy "Your credit has been approved" to the sad news that "Your credit has been cancelled." The letters ask for information, provide information, and solve problems. In some letters you guide your reader quietly to your point (couch the distasteful news in the middle of your letter), and in some you speak directly and definitively: "We will ship when your check clears." In these cases you as the writer must assume the "recipient's" attitude: How would *you* react if you received the letter you had just written?

CHAPTER *2*

How to Write Successful Collection Letters

The purpose of a collection letter is to collect money while retaining the goodwill of your customer. A slam-bang technique of collecting may get your money in a hurry, but at the same time it will drive away business. You can ill afford that because you need those dollars for your operations. You *must* retain the goodwill of your clientele.

One seller found ignoring that truth detrimental to his reputation. He sold and installed some decorative iron work. The buyer, when making payment, held back a small amount because of a dispute over part of the installation. Within a week the supplier phoned, called the buyer a cheat, and threatened to file a lien against the property and even to tear out the installed iron work. The purchaser eventually settled, but he had already spread the word about that mean and stingy vendor. This is an extreme example, but when you write a collection letter, keep in mind the profits to be derived from goodwill.

BUSINESS VS. CONSUMER COLLECTION LETTERS

Retaining the goodwill of the debtor is especially important in collection letters directed toward individual consumers or businesses managed by one or two persons. An early collection letter to a larger firm, however, need not put as much emphasis on empathy with the reader.

In the early stages of business-to-business letters, the most important thing is to identify exactly what is past due. The letter should include at least the following facts:

The delinquent's order number and date.

The items purchased.

The seller's invoice number and date.

The dollar amount past due.

The original due date.

These items are essential to the reader in identifying the past due invoice.

Do not, however, construe this functional approach to mean that politeness, fairness and consideration for the reader can be ignored. The primary difference is that in a business collection letter you must provide more technical identification of the delinquent item than is usually necessary in a consumer collection letter.

THE TONE OF COLLECTION LETTERS

A collection letter is a letter of persuasion. You are urging the reader to pay past due bills. Persuasion is best accomplished with an indirect approach that attempts to change a resistant mind or a negative attitude. This can be done by telling your reader the direct benefits of paying promptly. These benefits include maintaining self-interest and a good reputation, having a good credit rating, and being relieved because a debt is paid.

Consider how your reader will react to the words you use in your letter. This is often referred to as the "you" attitude. The better you come to know your reader, the better you can word your letter to get the desired reaction.

Even collection letters must be friendly and polite—all the way through the collection process to turning the account over to a legal agency. For example, do not write, "We already mailed you a statement and a courteous letter," but employ a little real courtesy by saying, "In case the statement we mailed October 3 did not reach you, we are enclosing another one. We hope to hear from you soon."

Although in a collection letter you must assert your right to past due payments, an aggressive approach must be toned down, especially in the early letters. The early letters should be reminders. An aggressive first letter will insure that the debtor returns his unwritten check to his desk drawer.

It is often tempting for a creditor to state or suggest ways in which a debtor could improve his or her business operations, hoping that that will reduce delinquent payment periods. These suggestions are inadvisable unless, at a later time, the debtor asks for or implies that some help would be appreciated. Help can then be given by a supplier who prefers to work closely with a debtor rather than to cut off a potentially profitable customer.

Always assume that the debtor will pay. This can be suggested with comments such as, "Open credit will be available again as soon as we receive your payment," or, "We are enclosing a brochure illustrating our fall line of women's dresses," or, "Your past cooperation is appreciated."

Never write a threatening collection letter unless you have a specific plan for carrying it out and you then follow through when the circumstances warrant. Idle threats by a creditor are not idle words in the view of the debtor. The possible legal repercussions must be considered.

SUGGESTIONS FOR EFFECTIVE COLLECTION LETTERS

A nearly unlimited number of suggestions could be made to help you write better letters. The primary advice is to address your letter to the decision maker. That will result in faster action than by sending the letter to the department involved. It will end up there, but with direct instructions from the responsible person. With word processors, even form letters can be processed individually. The recommendations listed here will not fit every situation, but you will find a quick review of them beneficial when you start to write your collection letter.

1. Start collection procedures immediately after the account becomes delinquent.
2. Let your reader know in the first sentence that this is a collection letter.
3. Be persistent. Keep at it. "The squeaky wheel gets the grease."
4. Make collection letters brief, but not curt.
5. Avoid stilted language. Be clear. Be specific.
6. Be firm but reasonable.

7. Be kind, helpful and respectful.
8. Be friendly and sympathetic.
9. Always retain your customer's goodwill.
10. Treat your reader as an honest person.
11. Appeal to the individual interests and feelings of your readers. Consider their points of view.
12. Never lower yourself by displaying anger, pity, contempt or malice.
13. Never repeat an appeal made in a previous letter.
14. Provide a flexible collection plan.
15. Provide your debtor with a reason why it is to his advantage to pay promptly.
16. Make each successive letter stronger.
17. State the amount due in each letter.
18. Imply that the debtor will pay.
19. State how payment may be made.
20. Include the original due date.
21. Politely ask for payment—without apologizing.

TIMING OF COLLECTION LETTERS

The time interval between collection letters is determined primarily by the seller's credit policies. These policies should include answers to the following questions: Is the account profitable enough to permit slow payments? Will the account be profitable enough in the future to allow delinquent payments now? Are you in a cash bind? Is the economy booming or slowing? Are you selling perishable produce to a Mom-and-Pop grocery or road-building equipment to the Federal Government?

Time intervals normally vary from fifteen to thirty days and may continue for periods of from three months to a year before the account is turned over to a collection agency or an attorney.

HUMOR IN COLLECTION LETTERS

In collection letters, humor should be used sparingly and only with forethought. Although humor is important to a balanced life, not all people in debt respond well to the lighthearted. Consider the probable reaction of your reader before mailing a humorous note.

When humor is used, make the story short with a tantalizing rather than stinging point. Avoid expressing sarcasm, ridicule, irony or irritation. Light humor can be effective in first reminders for small accounts and as a device for getting attention.

For debtors whom you think will respond favorably, one version of an old standard that has been successful for more than forty years goes something like this:

> **Please send us the name of a good lawyer in your city. We may want to sue you.**

ATTENTION-GETTING OPENINGS FOR COLLECTION LETTERS

The opening of a collection letter must attract the attention and arouse the interest of your reader. The techniques for doing this are limited only by your imagination. Opening statements can vary from:

> **Just a reminder that we have not received your payment.**

to slapstick comedy:

> **"He wants my autograph—on a check."**

Other first sentences to awaken the reader include:

> **When they ask about you, what can we say?**
>
> **I am as embarrassed to write this letter as you are to receive it.**
>
> **Is our Fiery Kilowatt heater working well for you this cold winter?**
>
> **I am sure we both agree that a good reputation is essential to a prospering business.**
>
> **Again, may we call attention to your loan payment due March 30.**
>
> **Why haven't you paid? Why haven't you written? Why haven't you phoned?**
>
> **Could you tell us why you haven't paid your account?**
>
> **We cannot in good conscience carry your account any longer.**

STRONG CLOSES FOR COLLECTION LETTERS

The end of a letter is its most emphatic part; make the last statement or request strong and definite. Be *specific* about *what* you want, *when* you want it, and *how* you want it done. At the same time, keep in mind consideration for your reader because an offended reader pays slowly. Examples for specific purposes follow:

For Prompt Action

In order to open your account for further purchases, please let us hear from you today.

To avoid additional expenses and unpleasantness, we expect to hear from you within ten days—before August 12.

Because we are anxious to provide fast service, please let us hear from you this week.

We can help you just as soon as we hear from you.

To Build Goodwill

We are happy to cooperate with you, and look forward to serving you for many more years.

Thank you for bringing the problem to our attention. We are always glad to help.

We appreciate your cooperation.

Thank you for letting us help.

To Soothe

The mistake was obviously ours. We misunderstood your complaint. We have taken steps to correct the situation and hope you will bear with us for a few days.

We cannot disagree with your feelings; we would have felt the same in your situation.

We are sorry we had to take the action we did, but under the circumstances we had no alternative. We hope you understand.

This action may seem unnecessary at this time, but later I am sure you will appreciate what we had to do under the circumstances.

We would sincerely like to grant your request, but we are unable to do so now. We are, however, looking forward to serving you in the near future.

To Apologize

We are sorry for the inconvenience we caused you, and you can be sure we will make every effort to prevent it from happening again.

We feel bad about the trouble we caused you and hope you will accept our sincere apologies.

Thank you for calling the error to our attention so we may correct it. We are sorry for causing you the inconvenience.

Your patience is appreciated. We have corrected the cause of our mistake, and you can be assured it will not occur again.

To Reassure

We appreciate the business you have given us, and we trust you will understand that we cannot be of service to you at this particular time.

Of course we are sorry to have to turn down your request, but we look forward to serving you in future months.

We dislike, as all business people do, turning away a sale, but I am sure you understand why we must at this time.

A lost sale leaves us with an empty feeling, but, as you know from the circumstances, it is not possible for us to help you this time. The near future may look more promising.

To Repeat

Again, prompt payment will retain your good credit standing.

To repeat, the sooner we receive payment, the sooner we can help you.

Which of these two suggestions appeals to you? Please let us hear from you right away.

To prevent these added expenses and the inconvenience to you, please let us hear from you within ten days.

We can release this order when we receive your financial statement. Please mail it today.

To forestall bothering you again about this overdue balance, please mail a payment today in the enclosed envelope.

Repeated reminders are a lot of trouble for us and a bother to you. Please help us both by mailing your payment today.

Briefly, a partial payment of $____ will keep your account open.

To Promote the Future

Now that we have your financial statement, it will be a pleasure to approve your future orders promptly.

We are available to serve you at any time, so please call at your convenience. We will work hard to make you a happy customer.

We appreciate your prompt payment for your recent order. We look forward to more years of serving you.

Now that your account is on a current basis, we look forward to approving your future orders promptly. A continuing business relationship will benefit both of us.

COOPERATION WITH THE DEBTOR

The knack of collecting money is to work WITH the person who owes you. Offended debtors make a practice of paying slowly and eventually taking their business elsewhere. We know of one person who inquired about a statement showing $600 due when he could account for only $200. When questioned about what happened to a $500 payment made the previous month, the creditor exhibited strong aggravation and ranted on about slow payments. Not being able to get an explanation over the phone, the debtor asked for a detailed statement and told his bookkeeper to hold all payments until the following month.

Conversely, a friend told us of a collection agency member who collected a $30 medical account from an elderly southern lady. She appreciated his conduct so much that she cooked him a feast of turkey, turnip greens, sweet potatoes and a variety of home-baked breads.

Another technique for getting your debtor to cooperate is to omit words with an unfavorable connotation and include words with a positive feeling.

WORDS TO AVOID

cannot understand	delinquent
we insist	ignore

failure on your part	require
compelled	wrong
our demand	force

POSITIVE WORDS

respond	your payment
fairness	your check
you	mail today
your credit	please

FORMAT

As the letter writer, clearly identify yourself by having your name typed below your signature. Include your mailing address and telephone number or that of the company sending the letter. These make the response by the reader easier and quicker.

FINANCE CHARGES

Many collection letters in this book mention finance charges that are added to late payments. This can be properly done only when those charges are stated on the original purchase contract or invoice.

PAYMENT PROGRAMS

Another collection technique to use in conjunction with debtor contracts or payment programs is to mail two copies to the debtor, requesting that he sign one and return it with the initial payment. This provides the credit granter with signed evidence of the debt.

SIMPLIFIED ORGANIZATION

A special feature of this book which helps you organize your thoughts when composing a collection letter is the "How to Do It" section preceding each stage of letters. This feature is a basic outline for your letters. Using these steps you will remember all essential parts of your letter and eliminate unnecessary digressions.

For example, the "How to Do It" outline for a first stage collection letter is as follows:

1. State or imply that this is a collection letter.
2. Mention data relevant to the situation, what you are asking for, how the reader can be helped, and reasons for paying now.
3. Make the request for payment.

Notice how the two early reminder letters below follow this outline:

1. As one of our good customers, there must be a reason why your payments have gotten a little behind.

   Is there anything we can do to help or something we can correct?

   The amount due is $129.40.

   Please let us hear from you today.

2. Just a friendly reminder that your account has gone past the discount period and is now past due.

   If your check is in the mail, we say, "Thank you." If not, won't you please give this overdue invoice for $392.98 your prompt attention?

Part II

LETTERS TO CONSUMERS

CHAPTER 3

Credit Letters to Consumers

Credit letters to consumers cover situations from acknowledging a request to explaining your Non-Sufficient Funds (NSF) policy, from reactivating an old account to apologizing for your own error.

Welcome your customer when he sends you his first order. Thank him for his continuing business. Send him a "seasons greetings" letter. When appropriate, send him a letter of concern or special recognition.

Letters addressed to individuals show empathy with the reader, a feeling of caring, a touch of personal friendliness. While remaining friendly, letters to large organizations need more detailed identification of the problem being discussed.

Customers and clients do business with people they like. Your letters reflect you. Let your correspondence portray optimism, courtesy, and goodwill.

HOW TO DO IT

1. Reveal the purpose of your letter in the first sentence.
2. Add any needed clarification.
3. Offer a solution.
4. Ask for cooperation.

New Account Invited

Dear Mrs. Conrad,

Welcome to Lodi. We understand you have recently moved here. You will find this community friendly and fast-growing.

Banner's Department Store opened just last week at the new Rancho Shopping Center. We would like to welcome you as an open account customer. Please return the enclosed application or stop by to visit us in person.

Sincerely,

Dear Mr. Bollen,

Welcome to __city__. We would like to introduce you to Speller's Sporting Goods. We feature only national brands at the most reasonable prices.

Most of our customers enjoy our 30-day open account. Just fill in the short application form enclosed. We anticipate having you join us.

The fishing season opens next month. We can get you ready.

Sincerely,

Dear Mr. MacArthur:

We consider you one of our best customers, and we would like to THANK YOU for your patronage. Today we have a new, exciting service to offer and thought you should be the first to know.

During our last thirty-two years of business, Symons True Value has constantly sought new ways of serving you. We have always tried to offer the latest in service and merchandise. This fine tradition of quality service makes us proud to offer you the new TRUE VALUE CHARGE CARD.

The benefits of the TRUE VALUE CHARGE CARD are:
   The card is free: there is no annual fee.
   Easy payment terms: you have 25 days after your monthly billing to pay your balance interest-free (this can be 45 days or more from the date of your purchase).
   Low installment payments: if you choose, only five percent of your balance needs to be paid each month (finance charges will be assessed after the first month).

Nationwide acceptance: the card can be used at thousands of participating True Value and V & S Variety stores nationwide.
Leave your card: if you choose to use your card only at Symons True Value, we have established a safe way for you to leave your card at the store.

Symons True Value is switching to a national charge system because it will enhance our ability to serve you, the customer. Because our business has grown substantially in recent years, we are able to offer credit card accounts to everyone living in this area.

How do you get your charge card? Just fill in the partially completed application. Please mail it or send it to us with your next payment. It takes only a moment. Use the enclosed postpaid envelope.

We value your business very much, and we feel this change will serve to strengthen our relationship in the future.

Thank you for your cooperation in making this change.

Sincerely,

CREDIT REQUEST ACKNOWLEDGED

Comments

Answer your customer's request for credit courteously and promptly. Take no chances that he or she will lose interest or forget, because competitors are just waiting for that to happen. Also, make your decision about granting or refusing credit as soon as possible and inform your customer immediately.

Dear Mr. Ralton,

Thank you for promptly returning your credit application. It is being processed now and you will hear from us shortly.

We take pride in the completeness of our window guard selection and in the promptness of our installation service. We specialize in wrought iron guards made to customer specifications—any size for any window.

Sincerely,

Dear Mr. Wisney:

Thank you very much for returning your credit application form.

We are making a few inquiries and will let you know the results just as soon as possible.

When you can, please visit our store to acquaint yourself with our wide range of merchandise and our friendly service.

Sincerely,

BANK DATA REQUESTED

Dear Mr. Herbst:

Mrs. Wallace A. Orlone of ___(address)___ has given your bank as a credit reference.

Could you provide us with her recent average checking and saving balances and any loan experience with her?

We thank you for your effort and will reciprocate at your request.

An envelope is enclosed for your reply.

Sincerely,

Dear Mr. Gollan:

Re: Name _____
     Address _____
     _____

The above named person has given ___(your)___ bank as a reference. He states he has a savings and two checking accounts with you and that your bank financed an automobile purchase for him three years ago.

We would appreciate receiving his average balance in these three accounts and his payment record on the auto loan.

Sincerely,

BUSINESS DATA REQUESTED

Comments

When asking someone to give you their credit experience with your customer, make the reply easy. One good technique is to send a letter or form with blanks that can be filled in with a simple check mark or one word. Chapter 1 suggests twenty-three possible questions.

Enclosing a self-addressed, postpaid envelope is almost a requirement.

Dear Mr. Heiser:

John T. Peele has given us your company's name as a credit reference.

We would appreciate your giving us your recent credit experience with him. This information will be kept confidential, and we will reciprocate when you request data from us.
  A customer for how long?
  Amount of credit allowed?
  Pays promptly?
  Past due balance?
  Other comments?

Sincerely,

Dear Mr. Timko:

The following individual has applied for credit with us:
  Name _____
  Address _____

The information we are asking for will be kept strictly confidential, and we will gladly reciprocate.
  A customer how long_____
  High credit balance $_____
  Payments: prompt _____ slow _____
  Comments_____

Sincerely,

CREDIT GRANTED

Comments

When granting credit, you are happy and your customer is happy. Let this show in the first sentence. Mention your payment period and finance charges. It is also helpful to include a pleasant comment that will build sales goodwill, because this is the start of a new relationship.

Dear Ms. Kelly,

With pleasure we have opened a charge account for you. Welcome to our growing number of happy customers. We place emphasis on quality products and personal service.

Billings will be made monthly with a minimum amount due. Amounts held for future payments will include a finance charge of 1½% each month.

You will be pleased with our wide selection of merchandise.

Sincerely,

Dear Mrs. Kellock,

Thank you for requesting a credit card from O'Keefe and O'Riley. We are pleased to enclose your card today.

You will find shopping here a relaxing experience. Sales are made in a quiet and friendly atmosphere. Our quality speaks for itself.

Purchases are billed monthly, and you have thirty days to pay. After the thirty days a small one-percent-per-month financial charge is added.

Thank you for joining us.

Sincerely,

CREDIT LIMIT EXTENDED

Dear Mr. Hanson,

Because you are a valued customer, it pleases us to extend your credit limit to $3,000. Your good credit rating with us has qualified you for this higher limit, and it is available to you right now.

We feel sure you will welcome this new financial freedom now and the added convenience in the coming year.

Your business is a valuable asset to us, and we look forward to serving your future credit needs.

Sincerely,

Dear Mr. Gadsen:

You will be pleased to learn that your open credit limit has been raised to $4,300. We are able to do this because of the way you have managed your account in the past. We appreciate your business and your habit of making prompt payments.

We look forward to a continuing business relationship.

Sincerely,

TIME EXTENSION GRANTED

Dear Mrs. Healy,

Your frank letter of May 7, 19__ is appreciated. We realize that personal misfortunes sometimes occur. Considering your past record of prompt payments, we have no difficulty in extending your payment schedule.

May we suggest $150.00 per month for six months? At that time we will take another look at your outstanding balance and examine our future relationship more carefully.

Cordially,

Dear Mr. Gross:

A fire is an unexpected tragedy. Even when that contingency is prepared for, the immediate loss of income can be a harsh burden.

We wish to help where we can. We will extend your payment period for three months. At the end of that time we are confident that your financial recovery will be well on its way and that your regular payments can be resumed.

Sincerely,

NEW CUSTOMER WELCOMED

Comments

A letter welcoming a new customer is similar in many ways to a letter granting credit. Both are cordial and full of pleasant anticipation for both parties. You may include a little sales pitch. A new customer not cared for can soon be enticed away by a competitor.

Dear Mr. O'Connor,

Your credit rating is excellent, making us pleased to welcome you as an open account customer at Barron's Hardware. We carry only quality products and place special emphasis on our vast assortment of both hand and power tools.

Our terms are net 30 days from the monthly billing date. Finance charges are one percent a month on unpaid balances.

Notices of special sales will be mailed to you in advance, allowing you one day of sale shopping before our general announcements.

Sincerely,

Dear Ms. Nolan,

You are a welcome customer. Your credit has been approved to a limit of $1,500.00. This should take care of your immediate stationery requirements and can be adjusted as your needs increase.

As you know, we are expanding and will soon have a much wider selection of office supplies along with a more convenient floor layout.

Again, welcome.

Cordially,

FORMER CUSTOMER WELCOMED

Dear Mrs. Ingalls,

It is a pleasure to receive the order you phoned in yesterday. We are happy to hear from you again. We take special pride in keeping long-time customers and thank you for your renewed business.

The cookware you ordered is being shipped today.

Welcome back.

Sincerely,

Dear Mrs. Herwig,

You have not used your open account with Martin's recently. If the fault is ours, please write, phone, or stop in soon so we may make whatever corrections are necessary.

If you have merely drifted away from using our store, perhaps our annual fall sale that starts in two weeks will renew your interest. We will send you a notice, and we suggest you watch for our ads in the newspaper.

Our goal is to serve your needs.

Sincerely,

Dear Mr. Olinger,

Our greatest fear is that our customers may wander away. We notice that you have made no purchases in the last six months.

Is there a reason? Was there a disagreement with us? Did we fail you in some way?

Whatever the reason, we would be grateful for a brief comment at the bottom of this letter. You can use the postpaid envelope enclosed to mail it back to us.

Your response would be appreciated.

Sincerely,

_____

CREDIT DELAYED

Dear Mr. Lowry:

Thank you for your interest in Epper's Department Store and your request for a credit account.

We notice that you have been in this area only a few weeks and have just begun to work here. When you have lived and worked here a little longer and have established a bank account, we will be happy to review your application. We hope we can open a credit account for you when you apply again in another two months.

In the meantime, please take advantage of our Annual Sale next month. We carry lines of quality merchandise and are especially proud of our men's shop.

Please let us hear from you again.

Sincerely,

_____

Dear Mrs. Banner:

Thank you for your recent request for a charge account at Webster's. Your confidence in our store is appreciated.

Although we are not in a position to open an account for you just now, perhaps we will be able to do so when your residency has been established six months from now.

Meanwhile, please visit us often and enjoy the many conveniences of shopping at Webster's. Every effort will be made to serve you well.

Sincerely,

_____

Dear Mrs. Shannon,

Thank you for your credit application. We appreciate your interest in Spellman's.

We believe that in another six months we should be able to open an account for you. The number of your monthly payment obligations will probably be reduced by that time.

Until then, remember that cash purchases have no monthly finance charge.

Please contact us again in February.

Sincerely,

Dear Mrs. Ladden,

Thank you for requesting an Allen's charge account. We appreciate this expression of your goodwill.

As you probably know, a routine credit investigation is the usual procedure before new accounts are opened. Since the available information in support of your credit application is incomplete, we shall appreciate your assistance.

When you have a convenient moment, will you please stop in at or call the Credit Office on the second floor? No doubt you can furnish the information we need to reconsider your request.

We are looking forward to talking with you, and welcome this opportunity to meet you personally.

Yours sincerely,

CREDIT REFUSED

Comments

Writing a letter telling your potential customer that you are refusing credit can be considered distasteful or a real challenge. You are turning away business that may in the near future become profitable. On the other hand, your job is not to lose money for your company. Your goal is to get this

customer to pay cash until his credit worthiness is established. The trick is to say "No" in a positive way. You do this by saying "Yes" to something else—a layaway plan, equal service for cash, or the probability of future credit.

Chapter 1 discusses this challenging subject of refusing credit.

Dear Ms. Esthers,

We appreciate your request for a Golden Credit Card.

It is a standard procedure with all companies issuing credit cards to check on the applicant's past payment record. We have found that you usually require more time to pay than our twenty-five-day terms allow.

If we have not received current information, perhaps you could furnish us with the names of two or three firms from which you are now buying on credit. We will be happy then to reconsider your request for a credit card.

In the meantime, a visit to our store will acquaint you with our outstanding selection.

Sincerely,

Dear Mrs. Lindstrom:

Thank you for your recent application for a charge account at Fordham's. Your application has received careful consideration and we find that the information furnished does not meet our requirements for granting credit. Our decision is based on the following reasons:

Length of employment insufficient
No credit file

I regret we could not be more helpful at this time. Perhaps in the future, when circumstances have changed, we can again consider your request for a charge account. Meanwhile, our quality selections are available for cash, and you can take advantage of our layaway service.

Sincerely,

Dear Mr. Amos:

Thank you for your interest in Sander's Appliance Mart and your request for a line of credit.

Based on the information you supplied us and that from our normal sources, we are unable to grant you the open credit you requested. If you can supply us with additional references, however, and a statement of your financial condition, please do so, and we will be happy to reconsider our decision.

While waiting for this additional information we will welcome any orders accompanied by a cash payment.

Sincerely,

Dear Ms. Watts,

We appreciate your interest in Donaldson's Department Store and your application for a credit card.

Your lack of a permanent work record at this time prevents us from approving your application. Your part-time work references are good, and as soon as you establish a permanent work record we will be happy to reconsider granting you credit.

Sincerely,

Dear Mr. Conway:

Thank you for your order for two lamps.

We do not have any credit information about you, and therefore would like to suggest that you mail us a check for $189.50, including shipping charges. Or, if you prefer, we can ship C.O.D. via United Parcel Service.

We are glad to help you either way.

Sincerely,

CREDIT CANCELED

Comments

A letter canceling credit should be plain and to the point. By now your customer knows payments have been behind schedule. This letter will hold no surprises.

At the same time, keep the door open for the possibility of renewing credit privileges when conditions warrant. Both you and your customer will be pleased when that time comes.

Dear Ms. Bursett,

Because all your payments during the past year have been late, we must regretfully notify you that your credit at Brookfield Lumber Company has been canceled.

Our competitive prices and our well-known services, however, are still available to you on a cash basis.

Sincerely,

Dear Mr. Anderson:

Because we have had to constantly remind you of your late payments during the past two years and because these payments keep lagging further behind, it should be no surprise to you that we have, reluctantly, decided to cancel your credit.

When you become able to maintain your account on a current basis, we will work with you again.

For the time being, orders with cash accompanying them will be welcomed.

Sincerely,

MISUNDERSTANDING

Dear Mr. Waller:

At the end of June, our records showed that we owed you $270.00 *more* than your statement indicated was due, and at the end of July, we showed owing you $270.00 *less* than you showed due. The variance is $540.00. We have no record of invoices or credit memos for either amount.

Will you please check your records to see what you can find. Please let us know this week.

Sincerely,

Dear Mr. Veller:

There appears to be a misunderstanding about the due date of your first payment.

It was my understanding from our salesman, Mr. Boggs, that you were to make payments monthly, but you objected to a reminder letter sent on March 15 referring to a payment due March 1.

I know that in some instances Mr. Boggs makes agreements for the first payment to be delayed. What was your understanding?

I will contact Mr. Boggs and ask him to get in touch with you so you two can agree on when your first payment is due. That should clear the matter.

Sincerely,

NSF (NON-SUFFICIENT FUNDS) CHECKS

Comments

Checks returned by your bank can be redeposited and may clear the second time. If not, write and ask your customer to mail another check, to stop by in person to pay cash, or to mail a cashier's check or money order.

Be polite: any number of things could have happened, and your customer may be completely innocent of any carelessness.

Dear Mrs. Webster,

I am sending you a copy of your check that was sent to us from our bank on August 20, 19__ and was not paid because of insufficient funds.

This is your payment for August on your coat purchase. Will you please send us a certified or cashier's check? We will then return the unpaid check to you.

Sincerely,

Dear Mrs. Watson:

Your check number 324 dated June 7, 19___ in the amount of $98.29 has been returned to us by Western Bank.

Please stop at our shop to redeem your check. If that is inconvenient, you may mail us a certified check or money order for $98.29 to clear your account, and we will return your check.

Sincerely,

THANKS FOR PAYMENT

Dear Mr. Anson:

Thank you for your payment of $991.05. This clears your past due account.

We appreciate your cooperation and look forward to serving you again.

Sincerely,

Dear Mrs. Zeda:

Thank you for your recent payment of $126.00. Although the check was received a little late, your account is still open, and we hope to continue being of service to you.

Sincerely,

THANKS FOR FIRST PAYMENT

Dear Mr. Kloss:

Thank you for your first payment on your contract. We appreciate your promptness. Continued on-time payments will go a long way in establishing your credit record.

While paying off the contract, please enjoy your "houseful" of electric appliances.

Sincerely,

Dear Mr. Jocylin:

We appreciate receiving your prompt initial payment. Establishing a record of meeting obligations on a timely basis inspires us to try even harder to meet your needs. It also enhances your credit rating in the community. We thank you for your consideration.

Cordially,

THANKS FOR PROMPT PAYMENT

Dear Mr. Murrell:

A big thank you for the promptness with which you paid your furniture loan.

That has done much to establish your reputation for responsibility and your credit standing in the community.

Do not hesitate to use our store as a future credit reference. We will be pleased to help you.

Sincerely,

Dear Mr. Morinos:

We want to let you know how much we value your business. The prompt manner in which you maintain your account makes it a pleasure to do business with you.

We hope Johnson's can continue to serve your motoring needs for many years to come.

Regards,

THANKS FOR PARTIAL PAYMENT

Dear Miss Elka:

Thank you for your partial payment of $250.00. This leaves only $165.08, which will be due in thirty days. By making this payment on time, your account will be open again.

We look forward to having you as an open-account customer once more.

Sincerely,

Dear Mr. Rapp:

Your payment of $125.00 on November 10 is appreciated.

You know, of course, that you still owe $875.00. Your $1,000.00 balance has been overdue since July 30, and we want you to make regular payments of at least $200.00 every month. This should not place an undue burden on you.

Thanks again for your payment, and we are looking for the next one by December 10.

Sincerely,

THANKS FOR MAINTAINING ACCOUNT

Dear Mr. Horton:

Thank you.

You're the kind of customer Fraser's Store is proud to have. Your continuous promptness is sincerely appreciated.

Cordially,

Dear Ms. Godfrey:

This is the kind of letter we like to write. You have consistently paid your bills on time, and we wish to thank you for your cooperation. We hope to continue serving you for a long time.

Cordially,

CREDIT BALANCE IN ACCOUNT

Dear Mrs. Sheehan:

We are sorry you had to wait so long for us to clear your credit balance. Today, however, we mailed you a check for the full $47.45. Please accept our apologies for the delay.

Cordially,

Dear Mrs. Leddy:

Our statement of September 30, 19___, which is enclosed, shows a credit balance of $160.22. Would you like a check for that amount or do you prefer to leave it to offset future purchases?

Please indicate your preference at the bottom of this letter and return it in the enclosed envelope.

Sincerely,

    _____ Please send me a check.
    _____ Please apply the credit balance to future purchases.

Dear Mrs. Hudson,

The credit balance shown on the enclosed statement represents the amount <u>we owe you</u>. You may charge future purchases against this amount, or you may request a refund.

To obtain a refund, present the top portion of your statement at one of our stores or return it in the enclosed envelope. By either method, a refund check will be mailed to you.

Credit balances under $1.00 will be canceled after six billing periods. Credit balances of $1.00 and over will be refunded after four billing periods.

Thank you for shopping at _____.

Sincerely,

AUDIT BALANCE REQUEST

Dear Mr. Landt:

As part of our annual audit, we are required to verify our accounts receivable.

Our records show that on June 30, 19__ you owed us $402.57.

If that amount is correct, do nothing. If it is NOT correct, please fill in the correct amount below and return this letter in the enclosed business reply envelope.

We truly appreciate your cooperation.

Sincerely,

> Our records show $_____ owed to ___company___
> as of June 30, 19__.

> _____
> (signature)

Dear Mr. Bruno:

As part of our annual audit of Mercal Corporation, we must verify their accounts receivable balances.

Their records show that on June 30, 19__ you had a balance due them of $3329.47.

If you disagree with this amount, please indicate what your records show at the bottom of this letter and mail it in the enclosed envelope by August 15, 19__.

Thank you for your cooperation.

Sincerely,

APOLOGY FOR DELAY

Dear Mr. Hertel:

Thank you for your inquiry about your account balance.

We will mail this information tomorrow, and we apologize for not having gotten it to you sooner.

Sincerely,

Dear Ms. Cassedy:

We apologize for not sending our credit application form the day we received your request.

You will be pleased, we are sure, with the advantages of a line of credit: no cash to carry, no checks to write for each purchase, advance announcements of special sales, and a recognized credit rating.

We look forward to your application.

Cordially,

APOLOGY FOR LATE PAYMENT

Dear Mr. Brundage:

I wish to apologize in advance for being late with my payment due July 15, 19__. Certain unexpected problems have arisen, leaving me short of cash. This is a temporary situation, and I will be able to include the July 15 amount with my August payment.

I hope you will understand. There should be no further delays in my payments.

Sincerely,

Dear Mr. Andrus:

My August 31 payment was late, as you have undoubtedly noted by now. The $1429.80 due is enclosed.

The unusual problem causing the delay has been solved, and future payments will be made on schedule. I trust you understand.

Sincerely,

APOLOGY FOR UNINTENDED REMINDER

Dear Mr. Frye:

Your check and our reminder of an overdue amount crossed in the mail.

We hope you will accept our apology for being "trigger happy," and thank you for your payment.

Sincerely,

Dear Mr. Hyland:

Your account is NOT overdue as indicated in our letter of January 7, 19. There was an inadvertant delay in crediting your account.

Please accept our apologies, and we will do our best to avoid such annoyances to our prompt-paying customers in the future.

Sincerely,

EMPLOYMENT VERIFICATION

Dear Mr. Brinker:

Your employee, ___(name)___, has applied for credit with us.

Would you please verify his (or her) employment by completing the information requested below and returning it to us. A postpaid envelope is enclosed for your convenience.

Sincerely,

    Starting date:
    Monthly salary or wage:
Information provided by:
    Name (please print):
    Signature:
    Title:
    Date signed:

Dear Mr. Bassett:

Re: ___(name of employee)___

The above named person has applied for a home loan. We would appreciate your answers to these questions:
    Date employed:
    Present salary or wage:
    Likelihood that employment will continue for several years:

Please return one copy of this letter to us in the enclosed envelope.

Sincerely,

CREDIT INFORMATION REQUESTED

Dear Mrs. Tallion:

In reviewing your credit file we find that you apparently have changed banks. Could you please provide us with the following information:
Your current bank's
Name:
Address:
Checking account number(s):
Saving account number(s):

Your cooperation is greatly appreciated. A return envelope is enclosed for your convenience.

Sincerely,

Dear Ms. Cornett:

To keep our credit files current, could you please furnish us the information listed below:
Credit Cards
Name   Address

Mortagee Holder
Name   Address

Loans
Lender   Address

Thank you for helping us to serve you better.

Sincerely,

HOLIDAY GOODWILL

Dear Mrs. Bassart:

We seem to rush all year, often forgetting the personal friendships that are the basis of our customer relationships. During the Holiday Season, we take pleasure in exchanging cordial greetings and goodwill with our friends.

In this spirit, thank you for making our association with you pleasant during the year.

Cordially,

Dear Mr. Ritter:

As the magic of the Holiday Season approaches, our thoughts turn to those who have made our progress possible. We wish to express our appreciation for your goodwill—the very foundation of business success. In the spirit of friendship, we send you our hope for a continuing business relationship and best wishes for an enjoyable Holiday Season.

Cordially,

CONDOLENCE

Dear Mrs. Gooding:

May we offer a quiet expression of our sympathy to you and your family.

You are in our thoughts.

With Sincerity,

Dear Mrs. Capitelli:

Your great loss has saddened my staff and me. We wish to express our deepest sympathy to you.

Cordially,

ANNIVERSARY THANKS

Dear Mr. Moller:

Your order No. 444 was received exactly one year after your first order. It's a happy anniversary for us and we hope for you too.

We have tried to provide top-grade products and efficient service. If, however, you have any suggestions for improving these during your second year with us, please feel free to mention them to us. Our customers come first.

Cordially,

Dear Mr. Ebert,

Twenty years ago this month, you opened an account with us. A hearty "thank you" seems so little, but it does express our appreciation for the opportunity to be of service to you all these years.

Sincerely,

CHAPTER 4

Reminder Collection Letters to Consumers

A consumer collection letter is one written to an individual who purchased merchandise or service for personal consumption. To be effective, the letter must have a human touch, a feeling of warmth. Because of the necessary preciseness, letters to large firms often have an unintended coolness. Avoid this in consumer letters.

Reminders and first collection letters are informal memory joggers. No pressure is needed. Humor is often effective, but care must be taken to keep the humor neutral. Do not offend any particular group of people.

REMINDERS

The following reminders have proved to be effective when written with felt pen on invoices and statements mailed as soon as payment was overdue. Some of these words and phrases are available as stickers or on rolls of self-adhesive tape that can be purchased from stationery stores. Don't get carried away with the informality and humor implied by these reminders lest you actually write, "If you die, can we be your pallbearers? We carried you through life and would like to continue."

Second request

Please

Please pay

Please pay now

Please pay—this bill is overdue

Please send payment

We missed your payment

Have you forgotten?

May we have your check today?

Overlooked?

Just a reminder

$1\frac{1}{2}\%$ finance charge on past due accounts

Friendly reminder—payment overdue

If payment has been sent, we thank you

Past due—please pay

Thank you

Thank you for prompt payment

Is there a reason for not paying?

25% payment will be appreciated if you cannot pay in full today

This account is now overdue

Overdue—please pay this month

Could you make a 20% payment on this?

PAY

FIRST COLLECTION LETTERS

If one or two reminders don't do the job, the next step is to write a first-stage collection letter. This is still basically a reminder. It should be a friendly suggestion that payment is late. Your reader should know after reading the first sentence, however, that it is a collection letter. Make your presentation straightforward and simple. A longer letter that includes explanations and appeals can be put off until the third letter.

HOW TO DO IT

1. State or imply that this is a collection letter.
2. Mention data relevant to the situation: what you are asking for, how your reader can be helped, and reasons for paying now.
3. Make the request for payment.

JUST A REMINDER

Dear Mrs. Addams,

Just a routine reminder that you may have forgotten about your account with Dillsworth. Will you please send us your check today? The amount owed is $347.50.

Cordially,

Dear Ms. Keyes,

Just a reminder that your subscription to _____ will expire with the March 19__ issue. To continue receiving our expanded coverage, please send $28.00 for one year.

Sincerely,

Gentlemen:

Just a friendly reminder that your account has gone past the discount period and is now past due.

If your check is in the mail, we say, "Thank you." If not, please give this your prompt attention.

Sincerely,

Dear Mr. Ballard:

Just a friendly note to let you know we are still waiting for the next payment on your account. An envelope is enclosed for your convenience.

Remember, too, about our new, wide selection of Oxnard power tools, designed especially for home workshops.

Cordially yours,

    Amount due: $227.55
    Date due: November 30, 19___.

Dear Mr. Jeter:

This is a reminder that on June 1 a new carrier began delivering your Daily News. His name is John Simon.

If you have not yet sent in your June payment, please do so as soon as possible. Mr. Simon is an independent business man and not an employee of the Daily News.

If you have already paid, thank you for your promptness.

Sincerely,

Dear Ms. Wilfred:

Many of our customers are glad to receive a reminder that they may have overlooked a bill. Your last purchase in the amount of $399.76 is overdue. We would appreciate your mailing us a check today.

Cordially,

Dear Ms. Cronkite:

Will you accept our friendly reminder? Your account with us is now overdue. We trust you will make a payment of $34.95 soon. Why not today?

Cordially,

Dear Mrs. Crane:

This is a friendly reminder that your $129.07 account at Hallson's is fifteen days past due.

Could you please attend to this delay today?

Cordially,

Dear Mrs. Dumas:

Sometimes checks and reminders to send them cross in the mail. If this is the case, we thank you for your payment. If this is not the case, we would like to remind you that a payment is due, and we would appreciate a response today. The amount due is $134.95.

Cordially,

Dear Mr. Prindle:

Just a friendly reminder of your unpaid balance of $357.70. If you have recently mailed a payment, please disregard this note. If you have not mailed your check, we would appreciate your doing so today.

Sincerely,

Dear Mr. Knowlton:

Could it be that the check you wrote is still lying on your dining room table waiting to be mailed? If so, please send it on to us. If, however, you did send your check for $327.80, we hope you don't mind this friendly reminder, and we thank you for your payment.

Cordially,

Dear Mr. Burki,

Occasionally statements we send out do get lost in the mail. If that should be the reason for the delay in making your $42.00 August payment, we have enclosed another copy.

We feel sure you will wish to pay it promptly.

Sincerely,

Dear Mrs. Barbour,

Ten days ago we mailed you a reminder that your account was past due in the amount of $288.10. We have not received your payment. May we again ask that you send a check today? Thank you.

Sincerely,

PAYMENT OVERLOOKED?

Comments

The "overlooked" or "have you forgotten" letter is a face-saving ploy. The credit manager knows that forgetting is really not likely. Presumably the debtor was short of cash on the due date and also when he received your earlier reminder notice.

Although known to both parties as a fiction, there is nothing wrong at this stage in the collection process with being kind enough to provide your debtor with a ready-made excuse.

Just a REMINDER, Mr. Rich, that you may have overlooked making the last payment on your account. A copy of our bill for $401.20 is enclosed. Please mail your check today.

Regards,

Dear Ms. Waite:

Have you forgotten the last payment on your loan?

The final payment is $266.25. Because your other payments were on time, I thought you would appreciate this reminder. Please use the enclosed envelope to send in your check for $266.25. May we have it today?

Sincerely,

Dear Mr. Lamb:

Could you have forgotten? Forgotten that your account at Walter's Men's Store is past due? The account is $116.23.

This is just a friendly reminder that a payment today would be appreciated.

Cordially,

Dear Ms. Mesker:

The year is almost over. Time seems to fly by unnoticed. Perhaps that is why you have not yet paid the $159.98 for your last purchase at Ender's.

Could you please mail your check today?

Sincerely,

Dear Ms. Romoser,

Customers have told us they appreciate being notified when their accounts become overdue. Usually their delay has been an oversight, and this may be true in your case. Your past due balance is $____. Please mail your check today.

Sincerely,

Dear Mr. Lorenzo:

We thank you for the business you have given us, and would like to remind you of the balance in your account that is now overdue. You may have misplaced our statement.

The amount due is $999.05. A check mailed today would be appreciated.

Sincerely,

Dear Mr. Oxman:

Did you perchance lay aside our last month's statement and forget to pay it? That happens occasionally, and we thought this memory jogger would be in order.

The amount due is $456.75, and a prompt payment would be appreciated.

Cordially,

Dear Mr. Fountain:

Your account shows a balance of $492.10, of which $191.10 is overdue.

We wish to call your attention to this possible oversight. Please mail us a check today in the enclosed envelope.

Sincerely,

Dear Ms. Gavin:

We have been wondering if something unusual happened to your check for March. Your checks have always arrived before the overdue date of the 25th of the following month.

If perhaps it was overlooked, we have enclosed a copy of your March statement. Why not mail your check today?

Cordially,

Dear Mr. Forger:

We agreed that your past due balance of $405.10 could be paid in five monthly installments of $75.00 each with a final payment of $30.10 starting March 10, 19___.

We have not received your first payment and assume your delay is an oversight.

Please mail a check today so we can be assured the agreement will be followed.

Sincerely,

UNPAID BALANCE

Dear Mr. Cyril,

We are enclosing a copy of your latest statement. As you can see, most of the items are past due.

We would appreciate at least a half payment today.

Sincerely,

Dear Mrs. Mayland,

The enclosed bill is a copy of the one previously sent to you. This is just a reminder that your payment hasn't been received.

Perhaps the original was overlooked, or your check is now in the mail. If not, let us know when we can expect payment, or, better yet, mail your check today.

Thank you,

Dear Mr. Filbert:

Our records show that your account has an unpaid balance of $674.22. This balance is from the purchases you made in April and May of this year.

Please send us a check for $674.22 today. Or, if you have already mailed a payment, we send you our thanks.

Your business is appreciated.

Sincerely,

_____

Dear Mr. Wolfe,

Your account shows a balance of $_____. This amount became overdue a month ago. We would like to ask that you mail a check today.

Sincerely,

_____

Dear Mr. Kingsland,

There is an unpaid balance in your account of $577.00. This applies to the air cooler you purchased July 29, 19___.

We are sure the cooler is serving you well and will continue to do so for many more summers.

May we have a check for the $577.00 now past due?

Sincerely,

_____

Dear Ms. Growney,

As we mail this reminder, there is an unpaid balance in your account of $128.50, which has become overdue.

If you have sent a payment, we thank you; if you have not, however, we would appreciate your mailing a check today.

Sincerely,

_____

Dear Mr. Cortney:

The amount overdue on your account is $77.40. Please have a payment mailed within five days.

Sincerely,

Dear Mrs. McColley:

Mailing us a check today for $122.69 will clear your overdue account and make additional charges available to you again.

Sincerely,

Dear Ms. Patrari,

Your _____card account with us is past due in the amount of $_____.

Please mail your check by _____, 19___.

Sincerely,

WHY THE DELAY?

Comments

In contrast to the "oversight" letters, these suggest slightly more concern. They offer various probable causes for the customer not having paid and ask that the real reason for the delay in payment be revealed.

Dear Mr. Potter:

I am sure there is a reason why you haven't paid your bill for $753.78 at Matson's Electric. It is now 30 days past due.

If you have been ill or out of work or otherwise unable to pay, we understand. We can extend your payments. We would, however, appreciate hearing from you so we can work out a mutually agreeable payment schedule.

Please use the enclosed envelope or call us at 000-0000.

Cordially,

Dear Mr. McElroy:

As you have always been one of our good customers, we feel sure that there must be a reason why your payments have gotten a little behind.

Is there anything we can do to help, or something we should correct? Please let us hear from you.

Sincerely,

Dear Mr. Penn:

On occasion we all seem to practice the art of putting things off.

Could this be the reason you have delayed making a recent payment on your account at Harvard's? We hope you will consider sending us a check, perhaps today.

Cordially,

Dear Mr. Bellevan:

We have not received your first payment, due two weeks ago. When you opened your account, I mentioned that I would be happy to answer any of your inquiries. Do you have any questions about your account? I am here to help. Please call or mail your check today.

Sincerely,

Dear Mr. Verde,

We have been waiting day by day for a check from you. May we hear from you, please, especially if there is a question about the door or the billing? Please call us or mail your check today.

Sincerely,

Dear Mrs. Mele,

When a regular customer gets behind in her payments, we believe there is a good reason.

Is there something wrong that we can correct? Is there some way we can be helpful? Please let us hear from you, so that we can work together to solve any problems you have.

The amount now owing is $228.98. Please call us or mail your check today.

Regards,

TERMS OF SALE

Dear Mr. Monroe:

Your terms, as you know, are net the 10th of the following month. Every purchase made in one month is payable in full by the 10th of the following month.

Right now $639.90 is past due.

We would appreciate a prompt payment.

Sincerely,

Dear Mr. Dolin,

We were pleased recently to open a charge account for you. Because your first payment is now overdue, we feel we may not have given you a clear explanation of our terms.

All purchases must be paid in full 25 days after the billing date.

Your unpaid balance is $_____. Please mail your check today.

Sincerely,

Dear Mr. Ludas,

We appreciate your business and offer this friendly reminder that accounts are payable before the next billing date.

Would you please mail a check today for $129.48?

Cordially,

Dear Mrs. Wing,

We appreciate receiving the payments you have made on your account. Under the terms of our 30-day, no interest account, however, the full amount due must be paid each month.

Your present overdue balance is $_____. Please mail your check today.

Sincerely,

Dear Ms. Underewood,

This is just a reminder that under our terms of sale your purchase of March 7 will be due and payable on April 7.

 A copy of the invoice is enclosed.
 Your prompt payment would be appreciated.

Sincerely,

SMALL AMOUNT

Dear Mr. Foss:

Your check for $24.80 has not arrived.

This may be a small amount, but all overdue amounts are meaningful to us.

Won't you please help us serve you better by mailing your check for $24.80 today?

Sincerely,

Dear Ms. Mahaly,

It may seem a bother to remind you of your past due amount of only $16.47, and it may seem a nuisance to you to pay such a small amount immediately. However, an early check would be very much appreciated.

Sincerely,

Dear Mr. Budlong,

Because the amount on your statement is so small, we wonder if you have forgotten it.

We thought this note would remind you of the $17.40 still due. Please mail your check today.

Cordially,

Dear Mr. Patari,

This is a reminder that your invoice for $19.70 for your recent hit-record purchase has become past due.

Please mail your check today.

Sincerely,

Dear Ms. Florio,

You have consistently paid your statements promptly, which causes us to wonder if your last statement was overlooked or if payment was postponed because the amount is only $17.90.

We appreciate receiving even small payments on time. Could you mail your check today?

Sincerely,

Dear Mr. Patten,

Like most of our customers, you probably pay your bills at regular intervals. We have enclosed a copy of your last statement, and the amount seems so small you may have passed it by.

It would be much appreciated if you would mail your check for $12.95 today.

Sincerely,

Dear Mr. Conklin,

It's easy to misplace or overlook a small bill of only $11.40. We wonder if that is what happened to our statement of July 12, 19__, now 20 days overdue.

Would you please take a look, and if you have not mailed your check, please do so today. Your cooperation is appreciated.

Regards,

PARTIAL PAYMENTS

Dear Mr. Levy,

As I am sure you are aware, the balance due on your account is $329.44. This amount should have been paid by April 23, making it considerably overdue.

Please let us know when you will pay, or at least start by making a half payment on your account. The enclosed envelope is provided for your convenience. Please mail your check today.

Sincerely,

_____

Dear Mrs. Steen,

The day after we mailed you a reminder of your overdue balance, we received your check. Thank you.

The amount however, covered only part of your balance due. Would you please mail us another check for $132.00? This will bring your account up to date.

Cordially,

_____

Dear Mr. Ramsburg:

Thank you for your partial payment. The balance is still overdue, however. Would you let us know your plans for making additional payments? May we expect another check this week?

Sincerely,

_____

Dear Mrs. Grosso,

Thank you for your partial payment on your July statement. The balance of $92.00, however, is now past due.

Please mail your check for the balance today. A postpaid envelope is enclosed for your convenience.

Sincerely,

_____

MISUNDERSTANDING

Dear Bob Rogers,

We would like to clear up an apparent misunderstanding about your payroll deduction authorizations to deduct for loan No. 1472, $70 and for loan No. 1483, $55, from each semimonthly pay check.

It is approved procedure and standard practice throughout the corporation to make these deductions mandatory after deductions for payroll taxes, worker's compensation, and union dues. If this leaves you with a negative paycheck, Form C-111 can be signed by the plant payroll clerk as explanation for a smaller credit union deduction.

We must insist that payroll deductions be started again because your loan payments are now seriously past due.

Sincerely,

Dear Mr. Gettrich:

The second payment on your installment account is now overdue.

This may be because of a misunderstanding about the timing of your payments. You initial payment was due two months after the purchase date, with monthly payments thereafter. It is understandable, however, if you assumed you were to pay at two-month intervals.

Please mail your second payment today and then plan to send regular monthly checks to arrive by the 5th of each month.

Sincerely,

CHAPTER **5**

Request Collection Letters to Consumers

Second stage or request collection letters to consumers are slightly more direct than the first letters, but are still considered reminders.

In your letter, mention that it is a second reminder, that your customer did not respond to your first letter, or that you wish to remind him or her again of the overdue account.

An inducement to make additional purchases may be included. You may also mention a new item or service or upcoming seasonal special, or perhaps emphasize the quality of your merchandise or the length of time your firm has been serving customers.

Keep the style and tone of your letter informal.

HOW TO DO IT

1. Mention or imply that this is a second reminder of an overdue account.
2. Include a possible reason why the payment has not been paid.
3. State the amount due.
4. Ask for prompt payment.

SECOND NOTICE

Dear Mr. Kelso,

This is our second notice that your statement balance of $152.98 was due March 19, 19___. It is now 30 days past due.

Please mail your check today.

Sincerely,

Dear Mrs. Moody,

This is our second letter reminding you of your overdue bill. We believe you find, as we do, that things put off until later eventually become burdensome.

Both you and we would feel relieved if you would mail us a check right away for $292.22.

Cordially,

Dear Mrs. Gowan:

May we remind you again of the $195.40 you owe us for patio furniture purchased in April?

A check mailed today would be appreciated.

Sincerely,

Dear Mr. Shriver:

Since our first reminder that your account was past due, we have allowed you to make additional purchases.

The amount you now owe is $284.50, with $190.00 of that beyond our terms of net 25 days.

A check mailed today for at least $190.00 will be appreciated.

Sincerely,

Dear Mr. Hamm:

We reminded you two weeks ago of some invoices you had not paid. If you have not yet cleared them for payment, will you please do so now. The total due is $239.40.

Prompt payment will be appreciated.

Sincerely,

Dear Ms. Dirksen,

Did you misplace the reminder we sent you May 10? Your account is quite a bit overdue now. Because we are sure your delay is not intentional, would you please mail your check for $195.07 today?

The enclosed envelope is for your convenience.

Sincerely,

Dear Mrs. Carroll,

Although we sent you a reminder letter fifteen days ago, we have not received your check or an explanation for not paying.

We would appreciate a payment from you made today and your assurance that future installments will reach us on time.

You now owe two payments totaling $120. Please mail your check today.

Sincerely,

Dear Mrs. Carrico,

A friendly reminder (number two) that your unpaid balance is still past due.

Please mail your check along with a copy of our bill in the enclosed envelope today.

Thank you,

Dear Mr. Lindsey:

We reminded you two weeks ago of your past due balance of $_____.

If you have not already mailed a payment, please do so today.

Sincerely,

Dear Ms. Hegelson:

Our first reminder that $329.80 in your account was beyond the due date did not result in our receiving a payment.

We hope you will respond favorably to this second reminder. Please mail your check today.

Sincerely,

Dear Mrs. Ward:

Again we ask for a payment on your account, which became past due on May 1, 19__.

The convenience of our charge account is available only to those who pay within our stated terms of 25 days from the billing date.

The amount overdue is $129.40. Please mail your check today.

Sincerely,

Dear Mr. Maurer:

Did our first reminder go astray? Did you overlook the reminder that your account balances of $991.20 should have been paid by March 31, 19__?

A payment made today would be appreciated.

Sincerely,

Dear Mr. Lamka:

This is a second reminder that we have not received your payment due October 15, 19__. The amount past due is $_____. Please mail your check today.

Sincerely,

CREDIT LIMITED

Dear Mrs. Schnell,

Bringing your account up to date will keep your holiday buying from being limited.

With the festive season approaching, you will soon be thinking of your winter shopping. We have been stocking our store in anticipation of your needs.

A prompt payment of $391.57 will put your account on a current basis. Please mail your check today.

Sincerely,

Dear Mrs. Jordan:

You did not respond to our first reminder of your overdue account. Our new line of furniture started arriving yesterday, and we know you will love to browse through the wide selection.

To avoid having your credit limited, making this fine furniture unavailable to you, please mail your check for $_____ today.

Sincerely,

Dear Mr. Henry:

Placing a limit on the amount of your purchases, especially at this time of the year, is not a happy thought. This can easily be avoided by your making a payment of $430 or more on your account by November 20. That will clear the past due amount.

May we have your check today?

Sincerely,

SMALL BILL

Dear Mrs. Ansell,

It's easy to forget a small bill. If you have already sent payment for your one-year subscription to _____, we thank you.

If you have forgotten or misplaced our first invoice, please mail your payment with the accompanying invoice using the postpaid envelope enclosed.

By making your payment today you can insure not missing one copy of _____ and all the practical benefits its articles reveal.

Please help yourself by mailing your check today.

Sincerely,

Dear Mrs. Cordell,

Small bills are easily forgotten. If you have already sent the payment for your August purchases, we thank you.

If you have forgotten or misplaced our first invoice, please mail the upper portion of the enclosed copy of our statement with your check.

Your check mailed today in the postpaid envelope enclosed will clear your account.

Sincerely,

Dear Mr. Berning:

We acknowledge for a second time that bills as small as $22.50 are easily misplaced or overlooked.

Our statement of July 12, 19__ is now 40 days past due. Would you please check again to see if you have paid this statement? A copy is enclosed.

If the statement was not paid, we would appreciate your mailing a check today.

Sincerely,

Dear Mr. Albert:

Earlier this month we mailed you a reminder that your last payment was $6.00 short of clearing your account.

We would be grateful for a payment mailed today.

Sincerely,

Dear Mr. Smith:

Although your account has a past due balance of only $7.50, we find it necessary to send you a second reminder.

We feel a prompt payment is in order. It would be appreciated if you would mail your check today.

Sincerely,

IS THERE A PROBLEM?

Dear Mr. Wells:

Your statement is now 30 days past due. Your prompt attention will be appreciated.

If you have any questions concerning your account, please call 000-0000. If not, please mail your check today.

Sincerely,

WE NEED YOUR HELP

.... because your account remains unpaid and we haven't heard from you. Until we do, we must ask that you discontinue the use of your credit card until the minimum payment of $_____ is received. We regret the inconvenience and hope it is only temporary.

If there is a problem, please let us know, because the balance is substantial and we would like to work something out with you. If full payment has been sent, there is no need to get in touch with us. If not, please call or mail your check today.

Thank you,

___(name)___
___(address)___
___(account number)___

Dear Mrs. Ethelbert,

For more than three months we've sent you monthly issues of *The Easy Gardener*. But to date we haven't heard a word from you or received your payment or any indication that *The Easy Gardener* doesn't meet your needs.

If we don't hear from you soon, we'll have to suspena your subscription.

But there's a simple solution.

Take a moment right now to return the enclosed copy of our invoice with your check so we can continue your subscription.

This way you can keep on profiting from *The Easy Gardener*.

Please do it today.

Sincerely,

Dear Mrs. Asleson,

Have unforseen circumstances kept you from paying your account at Warren's? If this is true, a moment of your time to explain the situation and to let us know when you can resume making payments will help us. Although we received no reply or payment following our first letter, we are understanding.

If this should be an item that has been overlooked, a prompt payment of $489.90 would be appreciated.

Mail your payment today, please.

Sincerely,

_____

Dear Mr. Dubbles:

Because our reminders and first letter have failed to persuade you to settle your account, which is overdue in the amount of $187.50, it is possible that we are at fault.

If the problem is something we have done or not done, please let us hear from you so corrections can be made immediately.

If we are not at fault, you will agree, we believe, that an immediate payment would be appropriate. Please mail your check today.

Cordially,

_____

Dear Mrs. Stoltz,

Can we be of help to you in clearing the $205.47 you owe us? Your account is now 40 days past due. Because we did not receive a response to our statement and first letter, we believe there must be a reason for your not paying.

If there is a problem, please let us know so we can work together to clear your overdue amount. If there is no problem, mailing your check today would be appreciated.

Sincerely,

_____

Dear Mr. Ruckman:

May we remind you again that our records show an overdue balance in your account? The amount is $891.50.

Please let us know if we have been at fault in any way so we can promptly take corrective action. Otherwise, a check from you today would be appreciated.

It is a pleasure being of service to you.

Cordially,

Dear Mr. Waale:

Our records show that your payments are 30 days overdue in the amount of $_____. Is this amount correct?

Is there a problem that needs an adjustment? Is that the reason for your delay? If so, we would like to know so we can do whatever is necessary.

Your cooperation in responding to this second reminder would be appreciated.

An envelope is enclosed for your convenience. Please act today.

Sincerely,

Dear Mr. Rames:

It is unusual for us to write you other than to thank you for an order or payment.

Unless we are in error, your August statement was not paid on time, and we received no reply to our memo mailed two weeks ago.

We assume there is no error or problem. If you agree, please mail your check for $229.41 today.

Sincerely,

FAIRNESS

Dear Mr. Hutmacher,

Even after our first letter to you, we find a remaining balance of $298.98 in your account.

A payment from you today would be only fair; we too have bills to pay. Paying our bills on time keeps a wide selection of merchandise available for you.

Please mail your check today.

Sincerely,

Dear Mrs. Wershing,

We delivered your purchases the day after your order was received. Doesn't fairness suggest that you should make your payment within our normal terms of sale, which allows you 25 days?

Because this is our second request for payment, a check from you today for $679.50 would be appreciated.

Sincerely,

Dear Mr. Herwig:

We provide quick delivery and you pay promptly. What could be more fair?

We haven't, however, received a check for our last delivery, and we feel this second reminder is in order.

Your immediate payment of the enclosed copy of your bill would be appreciated. Please mail your check today.

Sincerely,

Dear Mr. Sheldon:

When we open an account for a person with your credit rating, we are certain that you will pay.

We are worried, however, because of a long-overdue balance. We offer only the best quality merchandise and service and believe that prompt payment is a fair exchange.

Please let us hear from you. The amount due is $_____. Please mail your check today.

Sincerely,

TRUST

Dear Mr. Asfahl:

Recently we had the privilege of opening an account for you. We feel the responsibility of providing you with quality merchandise. You no doubt appreciate the privilege of convenient buying and feel the responsibility of paying on time.

This is mutual trust, and we are puzzled that before your first payment has been made your balance is overdue.

We expected a response to our first letter, sent ten days ago. May we reaffirm our trust in you by receiving a payment today for $427.41?

Sincerely,

Dear Ms. Du Shane,

This is our second reminder that your July bill has not been paid.

We opened a 30-day charge account for you recently, trusting you to pay within our allowable 30 days.

We hope you will substantiate our trust by mailing us a check for $_____—today, please.

Sincerely,

Dear Ms. Coffield,

We trust you to pay your account, which, as you know, is past due, with a balance of $154.75.

We hope drawing your attention to this again will prompt a response.

An immediate payment would make us happy.

Sincerely,

Dear Mr. Starkey:

By granting you credit, we revealed our trust in you.

We believe this trust will be justified by your mailing us a check today for $232.10.

Sincerely,

Dear Mr. Lantz:

With only friendly thoughts, we again call your attention to your past due account.

We trust you will follow this reminder with a prompt payment, and in anticipation of that, we say, "Thank you."

Sincerely,

SMILE

Dear Mr. Quarve:

Doesn't the food taste better when your waitress greets you with a smile?

Here at ___(company name)___ we feel that collection letters should be presented with a smile. If our first effort was not successful, we will try again.

So, with smiles on our faces, we kindly ask for a reasonable payment today on your past due balance of $492.29.

Cordially,

Dear Mr. Allard:

We are still smiling, although you did not reply with a check or explanation to our earlier reminder, because we are confident you intend to mail a check before the end of this week. The amount due is $_____.

Sincerely,

Dear Mr. Morgan:

"Keep smiling," they say. We are trying hard to keep on smiling while waiting for $59.90 from you for the items listed on our statement of May 15, 19___.

A copy of the statement is enclosed. Please take a moment to write and mail a check today.

Sincerely,

ADDITIONAL AMOUNT DUE

Dear Mr. Imming:

Sometimes it is embarrassing and even disturbing to learn that you owe more than you thought. That is what may have happened since our first reminder about your unpaid balance.

You have continued to charge purchases since then, and additional amounts are now due.

Won't you please take action right away and mail your check today for $529.15?

Sincerely,

Dear Mr. Aikens:

Since our last reminder to you, an additional amount has become due. Are you aware of this?

No doubt you aren't, or you would have already sent a payment. While this is fresh in your mind, please mail your check for $397.20.

Cordially,

Dear Mr. Mercer:

We recently sent you our first notice that $_____ had been past due on your account since _____.

Accounts more than 30 days past due incur a one percent finance charge, with a minimum of 50¢, for each month your payment is late.

Please give this your immediate attention. We suggest mailing your check today.

Sincerely,

CONTRACT

Dear Mrs. Gathman:

Twelve days ago we sent you a letter requesting payment of your first installment, along with an explanation of the terms of the contract.

The first installment is now past due, and we wish to remind you of your obligation to make all payments according to the terms of the signed contract.

To continue our mutually satisfactory relationship, please mail your check for $397.00 at once.

Sincerely,

Dear Mr. Conety:

For the second time we find it necessary to remind you of your obligation to make monthly payments on the contract you signed with us.

Please mail your check today to cover the November payment of $425.00. The December payment will become due in two weeks.

Sincerely,

Dear Mr. MacCoy:

If you could make your contract payments no more than three days after the due date of the 12th of each month, we would both be spared the embarrassment caused by reminder notices and payment checks passing each other at the post office.

Please notify us ahead of time if you cannot meet a particular payment deadline. Kindly mail your current amount due today.

Sincerely,

Dear Mr. Dunmire:

We sent you a notice 15 days ago that the January 10 payment on your contract was due, but we have not received your check.

We want our business relationship to be a pleasant one and ask that you please mail your check for $308.00 today.

Sincerely,

COLLECTING FROM MILITARY PERSONNEL

Comments

The armed services cannot force their members to pay debts while in the military. However, the Department of Defense directs that they uphold moral habits and will aid you in locating service personnel. Call the nearest military base of the service to which your debtor is attached. They can direct you to their World Wide Locator section or its equivalent. Your providing them with the debtor's social security number will make their search easier.

If your letters to the military debtor do not produce results, one suggestion is to write to the debtor's commanding officer. This is essentially a letter asking for a favor, therefore you should be especially considerate and deferential.

Dear __(rank, name)__ :

Sergeant John Jones, Serial Number 00000000, owes us $_____ for the purchase of a TV set. Our efforts to collect have been unsuccessful, and the debt is seriously delinquent.

We would greatly value your mentioning this to Sergeant Jones, **not to** require him to pay but to remind him of his moral obligation.

Your assistance is truly appreciated.

Sincerely,

CHAPTER 6

Appeals Collection Letters to Consumers

If a reminder or two, and two letters haven't brought a positive response from your debtor, it is time to use the persusion technique. This technique is to appeal to one of a person's normal motivations. These motivations include sympathy, fairness, friendship, justice, duty, honor, loyalty, pride, fear, and self-interest.

Persuasion letters tend to be longer than others because you are building a series of arguments rather than stating bare facts.

It is helpful to offer a solution to your customer's problem. Perhaps you can suggest installment payments, smaller monthly payments or delaying the date of the first payment.

HOW TO DO IT

1. Mention previous efforts to collect.
2. Appeal to personal motivations.
3. Agree to help overcome your customer's difficulty in paying.
4. Press for prompt payment.

APPEAL TO CREDIT STANDING

Dear Mrs. Grau:

We have several times reminded you of your past due account of $676.24. It is now 90 days past due. Why have you not answered?

Not paying your bills on time can hurt your credit standing in the community. You can make time payments if you wish, and we will gladly work with you on a payment schedule you can afford.

Please restore our confidence in you and maintain your good credit rating by sending us a check now. Even a one-third payment will help.

Respectfully,

Dear Mr. Turner:

We have sent you several reminders about the $492.20 you have owed us since May 1. That was three months ago.

In consideration of your own credit rating, you should pay this amount now. Certainly you want to be fair to yourself.

Your check can be mailed in the enclosed postage-paid envelope. Please use it today.

Sincerely,

Dear Mr. Travis:

Dillon Company hates to keep bothering you with delinquency notes and letters, but your long overdue account is damaging your credit record. This is costing both you and us money. You are incurring additional monthly service charges and we are losing interest on uncollected funds. You could help us both by writing your check for $783.85 right now and mailing it in the business reply envelope today.

Sincerely,

Dear Mr. Bauman:

Your business and your goodwill—that's what we live by.

We want to help you maintain your good credit reputation.

If you wish, we can help you do this by arranging for installment payments of your past due $429.50. Please mail your check or contact us today. Let us share the spirit of cooperation.

Sincerely,

Dear Mr. Cordone:

When we opened your personal charge account, your credit references rated you highly. We see no reason to change that judgment. There must be some reason why your last statement has gone unpaid 60 days past the due date. The amount owed is $394.27.

We value your business and want to continue being of service to you and to help you retain your credit standing.

Let us hear from you soon. We will do all we can to help if you'll make a partial payment of $200. Please mail your check today.

Cordially,

APPEAL TO SELF-INTEREST

Dear Mr. McCann:

Your prompt payments on your open account in the past are appreciated by us. We hold in high esteem customers who maintain current balances. A sound credit rating will help make credit easier to obtain elsewhere.

Now, however, your payments are lagging. If there is some reason for this, please let us know so we can work together to bring your account up to date.

We are counting on hearing from you. The amount due is $628.72. Please call or mail your check today.

Sincerely,

Dear Mr. Allen:

As you probably know, retail stores in this area exchange information about the paying habits of their customers. This helps us when considering a credit application or a change of credit limit.

You are helped if you are a prompt-paying customer. Other retailers are more willing to offer you credit when we can report you as a "prompt payer."

Right now we would have a difficult time doing that, because your account is 60 days overdue in the amount of $428.90.

May we have your check today? We are sure you want the privilege of having credit available when you need it.

Sincerely,

Dear Mr. Wydman:

We could see you were pleased when you came into our store to purchase a reclining chair, found the one you liked, had it delivered three days later, and made no immediate payment.

That is credit at its best.

Because you want to retain the privilege of having a credit rating, we suggest you make a payment on your overdue account today; $150 would be a start.

Sincerely,

Dear Mr. Logue:

When you opened your charge account at Abram's, we had no apparent reason to doubt that your payments would be made promptly each month.

Now we find that even after several reminders and a couple of letters, your account is still sixty days past due.

As you may know, most stores in this area send reports of payment experience to the Retail Credit Bureau. We don't want to list you as a slow payer and are sure you don't want that either.

Only an immediate payment will keep you listed as a good payer. Please mail your check today.

Sincerely,

_____

APPEAL TO FAIRNESS

Dear Mr. Romas:

This is somewhat embarrassing: embarrassing to us because you are a good friend, and embarrassing to you because you owe this good friend some money—money that should have been paid long before now.

Some time ago (May 4, 19__) you purchased a chair from us, and we were happy to accept your promise to pay within 30 days. You seemed pleased with the chair, and I am confident it has given you many hours of comfort. Isn't it fair that you live up to your part of the agreement we made?

Let us be fair with each other. You have a comfortable chair. We would like our money. Since your payment is long past due, please make out your check for $491.75 and mail it today in the enclosed, postpaid envelope.

Sincerely,

_____

Dear Mr. Manor:

We expected an answer to the last of several letters we sent you. As you know, you still owe us $1591.00.

Truly, we are disappointed. I am sure you are not intentionally trying to make our work difficult, but that's what it amounts to. Is there some reason you have not paid? Some difficulty getting money? Too many other bills to pay? Let's make this easier for both of us. Call us, and we can solve any problems together.

We have been fair with you, and now we believe you will be fair with us. Please call or mail your check today.

Sincerely yours,

_____

Dear Ms. Cassity:

Most of our customers pay promptly. This enables us to provide wide selections and convenient services.

It is disappointing that you have not responded to our previous reminders of your past due balance.

We are confident, however, that you will send us a check this week for $802.45 so we can continue making our many services available to you.

Sincerely,

APPEAL TO FRIENDSHIP

Dear Mrs. Marshall,

We think of you as a friend as well as a customer, and we hope you feel the same about us.

We feel obligated to tell you that your payment methods are not meeting our expectations.

For some reason your payments are getting further and further behind, and an explanation would be sincerely appreciated. The amount outstanding is $499.06.

Please contact us today so we can work together on this; even better, send us a check today.

Cordially,

Dear Dave,

Because we have been friends for many years, I believe we can reach an amicable agreement on how to pay this account. How do you wish to handle it? Please let me have your suggestions or mail your check today. The amount due is $876.00.

Regards,

Dear Mr. Ehler:

If you are having difficulty making your payments at this time, perhaps we can help you by arranging convenient monthly installments. We are glad to assist in times of emergency or when unexpected obligations seem overwhelming.

Please feel free to discuss this with us by phone or letter or in person. You will find us willing listeners.

May we hear from you? Please contact us or mail your check for $929.40 today.

Cordially,

APPEAL TO COOPERATION

Dear Mr. Batten:

We are writing to you again to request your payment of $82.92 for the balance on your account. Because we have not received a reply from you to our past letters, we are concerned.

Please give this overdue account your immediate attention. We look forward to your cooperation. Why not mail your check today?

Sincerely,

Dear Mr. Cass:

You have not responded to our previous notices about your account.

Your balance of $591.40 is considerably past due, and we ask that you give this overdue amount your immediate attention.

Your cooperation would be appreciated. Please mail your check today.

Sincerely,

Dear Mr. Kugler:

Enclosed is a billing which indicates a third request for payment.

The end of the year is drawing near, and we expect your payment.

Please pay the balance due, $674.00 before the end of this month. That will clear both your books and ours for tax purposes. Even better, please mail your check today.

If you have any questions, please contact our office.

Sincerely,

Dear Mr. O. W. Oswald: Account No. 000-000-000

We are writing to let you know that we have closed your account and discontinued your credit card because the total amount owing remains seriously past due. We regret taking this action, but the lack of payment has left us no alternative.

We still want to help you, but time is running out. Please send the total amount owing today. If this isn't possible, call us quickly so we can work something out between us.

Thank you,

     Minimum Payment Due $_____
     Total Amount Owing $_____

Dear Mr. Hosler:

This letter is an appeal for your cooperation in clearing your past due account. We feel certain you will respond favorably with a check written today for $221.15.

Sincerely,

APPEAL TO DUTY

Dear Mr. Moran:

We hate to keep disturbing you, but $495.09 on your charge account is still past due. You owe us this amount, and we feel you are duty bound to pay it.

If you have a reason for not paying, please phone us or use the enclosed postage paid envelope to explain why.

If you have been merely putting it off, please mail your check today.

Sincerely,

Dear Mr. Nicklin:

Your buying and our selling is a transaction of mutual benefit, providing of course that our merchandise is satisfactory with you and that you pay as agreed.

We feel we should not have to wait any longer for your payment that was due over two months ago.

We would appreciate a check for $391.57 today.

Sincerely,

Dear Mr. Thrall:

We are concerned about your apparent indifference to our previous letters reminding you of your past due installment payments. Because we signed a contract, you are legally bound to honor the payment deadlines.

You are now two installments behind. We expect you to make your account current by mailing us a check today for $304.52, which includes late charges.

Sincerely,

APPEAL TO FEAR

Dear Mr. Bruce:

Your open account still shows the overdue amount mentioned in our recent letter dated April 27.

Won't you please send us the $287.20 today, so we will not have to consider other action for the collection of this amount?

We would appreciate your prompt payment. Today.

Sincerely,

Dear Mr. Motto:

You have been sent several notices and two letters reminding you of your past due bill of $629.32, yet we have heard nothing from you.

We are asking that you take positive action now to clear your account. We do not wish to involve you in any financial difficulties, but we must have a payment this week.

Sincerely,

APPEAL TO HONOR

Dear Mr. Beyers:

You will recall the recent letters we sent you on May 5 about your overdue account. Is a check for $379.80 on the way?

We allowed you the privilege of having an open account because you agreed to make regular monthly payments. We are asking now that you honor that commitment. If you haven't already done so, please mail your check today.

Sincerely,

Dear Mr. Neilson:

As reluctant as we are, we feel we must notify you, for the third time, that you are overdue in making payments on your account at Willistoff's.

An immediate payment of $297.92 will clear your account and your credit rating with us. A partial payment with a promise to make monthly payments of the balance will accomplish the same goal.

We look forward to a check for at least $90 from you dated today.

Sincerely,

Dear Mr. Fernald:

After reading your credit application, I thought, "There is a man whose word is his bond." I still believe it. I know you will pay your account.

However, since your last statement has not been paid and is past due, I would like to ask you to mail us a check for $329.40 today.

Sincerely,

APPEAL TO SYMPATHY

Dear Mr. Krugg:

Would you help us in our efforts to reduce costs? The reductions do get passed on to you. By sending your check for $579.90 now, we can eliminate the expense of writing additional letters and of carrying your past due account.

We hope you will mail your check today.

Sincerely,

Dear Mr. Hickey:

Your past due balance of $312.44 has been on our books for nearly three months. That is money that should have been in our bank and already used to buy more merchandise.

You can help us keep our costs in line by paying at least as much of your overdue amount as possible. We will work with you on arrangements for paying the remainder.

May we have your check for $80 or more today?

Sincerely,

APPEAL TO LOYALTY

Dear Mr. Luark:

PLEASE RETURN OUR CREDIT CARD

There is no easy way to ask customers to return their credit cards. We regret making this request, but your account remains past due despite previous efforts to obtain payment.

You have been a valued customer for many years, since ___(date)___, and we feel that your loyalty deserves special consideration. If you can send payment of $_____ today, please keep your credit card. This will assure continuation of your account. If there is a problem and you can't pay, call us and we will work it out together.

Sincerely,

Dear Mr. Daws:

You have been a customer of ours for many years, during which we have worked closely and pleasantly together. We supplied much of the material for the two additions you built onto your house.

This loyalty means a lot to us, but we feel it is becoming one-sided. In recent months your payments have not kept up with your purchases, resulting now in a past due amount of $528.00.

We would appreciate your coming in this week to talk to us about how you can reduce your past due balance. We can work out something together. Please call for an appointment or mail your payment today.

Cordially,

APPEAL TO JUSTICE

Dear Mr. Everett:

When you opened your account with us, we both understood that payments would be made within our terms of net 30 days, with one percent per month added to amounts carried over to the next month. Even the minimum amounts due must be paid each month. We are sure you agree that is no more than a just expectation.

We remind you again that you have made no payments for two months. To retain our cordial relationship, we must request a prompt payment of $895.00 to make your account current. Please mail your check today.

Sincerely,

Dear Mrs. Terre:

Frankly, Mrs. Terre, we are disappointed that you did not respond to our two reminder letters that your account is past due. The amount is $1195.90. The due date was 70 days ago.

It is costly for us to carry overdue accounts, and ultimately that cost is passed on to our customers.

We feel confident you will be fair and just and write us a check today.

Sincerely,

APPEAL TO PRIDE

Dear Mrs. Meadows:

When you applied for a charge account last October, you gave us three references. All three verified that you were "good pay."

Now, however, we find that you are three months behind in your payments. This is our third notice, and you now owe us $322.51.

We believe you take pride in your reputation as a good-paying customer.

Therefore, to avoid being on the record as "slow pay," please mail your check today.

Yours sincerely,

_____

Dear Mrs. Olson,

It is a disappointment to us that your account balance is becoming larger as your monthly payments become smaller.

Until recently your payments had been current, which leads us to believe there must be a reason for the change. As we suggested in two previous letters, please contact us to discuss these recent delays in your payment schedule. Some purchases are now 90 days past due.

We know you don't want the slowness to continue. We urge that you mail a payment today.

Cordially,

_____

Dear Mr. Raybould:

We greatly respect the high standard you maintained in the past for paying your bills on time. That was a help to us in serving you better.

But now we find that your last bill has remained unpaid for 60 days. Because we are sure you have not changed your normal practices, please let us know the reason for your holding back, or, preferably, mail us a check today.

Sincerely,

_____

Dear Mr. Wauters:

We appreciate that you always paid your bills before due. That was a high standard you set for yourself.

We are sorry to make this sound like the past, but we do so because your account has been overdue in the amount of $420.00 for over 50 days.

We know you want to return to your previous standard. You can do that by making out your check and mailing it today.

Sincerely,

FINANCIAL PROBLEMS

Dear Mrs. Bump:

We have not received a reply from you regarding the balance due on your account. We wrote you requesting payment of $429.90 on October 4, and have been waiting for you to get in touch with us.

If there is a problem, please let us know immediately. We can arrange a schedule for installment payments if that is convenient for you.

You can contact us by mail, or feel free to call us at 000-0000, but please take action today.

Sincerely,

Dear Mr. Lutz:

You have not made a payment on your account during the past nine months. We realize that financial conditions in your area may not have been good recently, and, accordingly, you have not been pressed for payment. By now, however, we feel you should be able to start paying again. We will be glad to work with you in making a reasonable payment arrangement on the $611.42 due.

Please call or write within ten days and let us discuss what can be done to get your payments started again.

Sincerely,

EXTENDED PAYMENTS

Dear Mrs. Miles:

I'm sure you are concerned about the $1,020.00 you still owe us on the bedroom furniture you purchased last March.

We can understand that problems do arise that prevent prompt payments and that possibly is why you have not kept up. If that is so, we can extend your payments if you will pay $170.00 before the end of each of the next six months.

We are sure this will be agreeable with you, and we are expecting a payment of $170.00 by August 30.

An envelope is enclosed for your convenience.

Yours sincerely,

Dear Mr. Dede:

We want your continued business and your goodwill as well as our money. At the same time, we can help you retain your good credit rating.

Your overdue balance of $927.00 may be a burden when you think of having to pay it all at once. We suggest you pay one half right now, and then set up a monthly payment plan you will feel comfortable with. Let us know what it is. We will work with you because we want to have you as a permanent customer.

Can you mail your first payment today?

Sincerely,

PATIENCE

Dear Mr. Meade:

We have sent you numerous letters requesting payment of the $407.00 open on your account since October 23. We have heard nothing from you.

Therefore, we must now insist upon an immediate payment. Please mail your check today.

Very sincerely yours,

Dear Mr. McCann:

You have not answered my previous letters requesting payment on your $822.00 purchase. We have received neither a payment nor an explanation for not paying.

I am sure you would agree that we have been extremely patient.

Could you kindly make a payment of $200.00? Please do so today.

Sincerely,

MINIMUM DUE NOW

Dear Ms. Peasley:

At this time we request that you temporarily discontinue the use of our credit card until we receive the minimum due.

We regret this inconvenience to a valued customer, but the minimum payment due is large, and we haven't heard from you.

Please mail your payment today or call us to work out payment arrangements.

Thanks for your help,

    Minimum Payment Due $_____
    Total Amount Owing $_____

Dear Mr. Picco:

We are recalling our card until the minimum payment due is received. As a customer since _____, you can keep our credit card by sending your payment now. If you can't, please use the lower part of this letter to tell us when you will pay.

Sincerely,

    Minimum due now $_____
    Total owed $_____

_____ Payment is enclosed.
_____ I can't pay until _____ and am returning your card to
you to hold until I get caught up.
_____ I will pay $_____ on _____ and $_____ each month.
Your card is enclosed.
_____ My phone number is _____.

TERMS OF SALE

Dear Ms. Weller:

May we remind you once more that our records still show your overdue amount of $992.47?

You are aware that all charges are due in 30 days.

Will you please let us know when we may expect payment? A check mailed today would be even better.

Sincerely,

Dear Mrs. Grambar:

We provide open accounts for the convenience of our customers to make their shopping easier.

To continue these open accounts it is necessary that they be paid within 30 days as agreed when they are opened.

As mentioned in our previous letter, your account is long overdue. The amount is $729.00. We are asking for a prompt payment. Please mail your check today.

Sincerely,

Dear Mr. Peterson:

I'm writing you about your charge account. It has been our policy to extend "temporary charge privileges" to our pharmacy customers who need medication and are not able to pay at the time the medicine is dispensed.

This temporary charge lasts until the next payday, or whatever other short-term arrangement is needed by our customer, but is to be paid within 30 days.

We have been negligent in informing you of what is outstanding, but would like to have the balance paid up to date. If this cannot be done, please contact us and let us make a workable arrangement to pay the charge on a scheduled basis.

According to our records you have an outstanding balance of $_____.

If this meets your approval, please mail your check today.

Sincerely,

Dear Patient:

Enclosed is an itemized bill for your recent hospital service. Your personal payment in full is now due.

We thought it would be helpful to explain our billing policy, which has been established to help contain hospital costs. If your account is not paid after 30 days, you will receive a series of reminders. If, after an additional 30 days, a total of 60 days, your account is not settled, it will be referred to an outside agency for collection.

We hope this explanation will answer your questions and encourage you to give payment of your bill your immediate attention.

If we can be of further service, you may contact your service representative at 000-0000. Otherwise, please mail your check today.

Sincerely,

DELINQUENT CHARITY PLEDGE

Once upon a pledge card . . . Mrs. Wasserman!

You promised your support to the Riverside Community Church Youth Building.

And then,
    the architects were called in,
    and a contractor found (we signed);

the cement arrived one sunny day,
the foundation was laid, solid and square.

The passers-by observed:
the floor that was poured
and troweled so smooth,
a two-by-four here,
a rafter truss there:
the roof was on.

Let's move in!
an office desk in that corner,
a class held here,
a meeting there:
a pot-luck supper is planned.

And then it happened—
we found that you were behind
in meeting your pledge—made
once upon a pledge card.

Now, what do you think we should do about that?

(signed by the minister)

Dear Ms. Linn:

Have you ever seen a hearse on the way to the cemetery towing a U-Haul trailer? It's true, "you can't take it with you."

You pledged $1200.00 to the Bell Health Foundation for the building and support of the Bell Medical Center. Many people—even you—are depending on the health care the Center will provide.

We received your first monthly payment, but nothing else has come for the past three months. Please bring your pledge up to date by mailing your check today for $300.00. The ill are waiting for your help.

Cordially,

CHAPTER 7

Final Demand Collection Letters to Consumers

The final collection letter to consumers is a letter of last resort. At this point, you are not as interested in retaining goodwill as in collecting money. Do not, however, push aside concern for your debtor with your direct language.

Mention the effects of not paying now, the loss of ability to get further credit, personal embarrassment, or court costs. Provide a deadline before which your reader can avoid these consequences.

If you mention turning the account over to an attorney or collection agency, failure to follow through if your customer does not respond to your letter may result in legal involvement.

For a strong impact with the final collection letter, you might replace the standard white paper with red paper.

HOW TO DO IT

1. Remind the reader of the delinquency.
2. Mention past efforts to collect.
3. Indicate consequences of not paying now.
4. Set a date after which the account will be turned over to an attorney or agency for collection.

FAIRNESS

Dear Mr. Steele:

You expect fairness from our company, and in turn we expect fairness from you.

Our collection procedures have been courteous and fair, with full consideration of your point of view and a willingness to cooperate fully.

To what avail? None.

This is our last letter to you before turning your account over to our attorney.

Only payment of the balance of $1472.80 *before* March 16, 19___ a can forestall legal action.

Very truly yours,

Dear Mrs. Idolovic:

The time for an agreement about the handling of your past due account is now.

We provided the services you requested, and you have made no complaints. It seems only fair that you should make regular payments, but our past requests have not prompted you to do so.

Your credit standing has already deteriorated and could be severely damaged. You have ten days to remedy this situation and send a check for $179.47.

If no payment is received by July 14, 19___ we will contact our attorney for possible legal action.

The enclosed envelope is for your convenience in making your payment today.

Sincerely,

Dear Mr. Bach:

We thought we were being fair with you when, in our last letter, we offered an installment arrangement to make payment of your overdue balance of $921.50 easier to handle.

We expected you to either agree with us or talk to us about your balance. But your reluctance to make any contact compels us to turn your account over to a collection agency or attorney.

We will do this in twelve days from the date of this letter if we do not hear from you in the meantime. Act now; mail your check today.

Sincerely,

Dear Mrs. Revson:

In our many letters and phone calls to you, we have assumed you intend to pay your outstanding balance of $1428.40.

We will continue to hold this assumption unless you cause us to change it. We wish to be fair, but we need your cooperation.

We would like to suggest that you call our credit manager at 000-0000, or stop by the office to talk to her. This will forestall stronger action on our part, but it must be done within the next five days, by March 21, 19___.

Sincerely,

REPUTATION

Dear Mr. Tasson:

Your account has been past due for so long and our requests for payment ignored for so long that we are now prepared to ask our attorney for help.

His action can only lead to inconvenience, added costs, and loss of reputation for you.

Only you can prevent this. We are willing to allow you ten days to reach an agreeable payment plan with us or to make complete payment of your debt of $2529.00.

Please contact us before March 28, 19___ or mail your check today.

Sincerely,

Dear Mr. Brieg:

On May 25, 19__ our legal department is scheduled to file a suit to collect our claim against you.

The decision to do this comes only after all other methods of persuasion have failed. To us it is a distasteful procedure, and to you it is a black mark against your reputation.

We want to give you one last opportunity to avoid litigation. You may do so by paying us in full no later than May 13, 19__.

Sincerely,

Dear Mr. Lancer:

If we were to take legal action against you to collect the $927.44 you owe us, it would seriously harm your credit standing and cause you embarrassment and expense.

That seems too great a price to pay for withholding payments. Because this is our FINAL attempt to persuade you to pay, please consider mailing a check today to avoid the possibility of litigation.

Sincerely,

CREDIT STANDING

Dear Mrs. Alden:

Your check for $498.80 must be in our office within ten days from the date of this letter, that is, on or before May 19, 19__, if we are to refrain from reporting your past due account to the Local Credit Bureau.

Such a report is a "black mark" against your credit rating and is seen by all the local stores.

This is a serious matter, and we anticipate you will respond accordingly. Please mail your check today.

Sincerely,

Dear Mr. Campion:

When you opened your charge account with Bonner's we anticipated a friendly and long-lasting relationship. We would make quality merchandise available, and you would pay on time.

This, however, has not been the case. You have permitted your account to become past due. Because our many attempts to collect have not received your cooperation, our next step is to turn your account over to an outside agency for collection.

This action can be prevented only by mailing your check for $902.43 within ten days of the date of this letter.

We hope you will respond favorably in order to prevent damage to your credit rating.

Yours sincerely,

Dear Mr. Mitros:

As you are well aware from our many requests for payment, your account with us has been past due for several months. This fact will have to be reported to the Regional Merchants' Association if we find it necessary to turn your account over to an outside collection agency.

To protect your credit rating, you must mail us a check for full payment of your account: $405.70. Your check must be received no later than February 12, 19__. This is your last chance. Why not mail your check today?

Yours sincerely,

Dear Ms. Wicks:

We tried.

We are trying now.

We don't want to have to try again to collect the money you owe us. Your payments used to be prompt, but this last bill is over a year old.

You have not replied to our earlier reminders, and now we must have payment by September 30, 19__. After that date we will turn your account over to a collection agency. To avoid that inconvenience and loss of credit rating, please mail your check today in the enclosed envelope. The amount due is $975.47.

Yours truly,

Dear Mr. Thornley:

In February we shipped the boat kit you ordered. We agreed, based on the credit references you sent, that you could have 45 days to make payment in full. Now June is fast approaching, and we have received neither payment nor response to our past due notices.

On June 15, we will make our "slow pay" report to the Retail Credit Association. With your name on that list, credit purchases would be extremely difficult to obtain. Ten days after the "slow pay" report, legal action to insure collection would start.

A full payment before June 15 will put you on an even keel again. Please take action today.

Sincerely,

NO RESPONSE

Dear Mr. Downey:

You were called on June 7, 19__ about your past due account, but you declined to accept the call.

Please mail the balance due, $378.90, today, or call us now. This will stop our planned procedure, which is to turn your account over to a collection agency on June 19.

Sincerely,

Dear Mr. Burney:

We have received no response to our recent letters reminding you of your past due bill for $499.90, not even when we mentioned that we might have to seek collection help from an outside agency.

Therefore, we see no solution other than to call our attorney for help in collecting the money due us.

Because this will take a few days, you have until December 6, 19___ to make a full payment or arrange a payment schedule with us. Please take advantage of this opportunity to clear your account. Please mail your check today.

Sincerely,

Dear Mr. Horine:

To all our recent reminders of your past due balance of $310.40, you have made no response.

Therefore, unless we have a reply within seven days, your account will be turned over to our collection agency.

A response by January 17 would be welcome.

Sincerely,

ACT NOW

Dear Mrs. Stanley:

We don't like to turn our clients over to collection agencies. Won't you please take care of the $266.60 you owe us NOW? Please mail your check today.

Sincerely,

Dear Ms. Crismond:

Immediate action is required of you if you wish to avoid the embarrassment, the inconvenience, the cost, and the loss of credit rating associated with court action to collect your overdue account.

We feel these problems are preventable, but your cooperation is essential. You must pay your account no later than October 20, 19___.

Please do so today.

Sincerely,

WAGE GARNISHMENT

Dear Mr. Webb:

If your overdue account in the amount of $345.45 is not paid within ten days, we shall be forced to turn it over to our attorney with instructions to garnish your wages.

You may avoid this damage to your credit rating by paying this debt within ten days, no later that May 12, 19___.

Sincerely,

Dear Ms. Draper:

Because your bill for $627.00 has gone unpaid for over a year, we have discussed a garnishment of your wages with our attorney. He says that is legal under state law and that we can proceed at any time.

We are, however, willing to give you twenty days from the date of this letter to pay the bill in full. If we have not received payment by then, March 27, 19___, we will start the garnishment procedure.

Sincerely,

INSTALLMENTS

Dear Ms. Seeley:

It shouldn't be necessary to send you another request to bring your contract payments up to date. Payment dates were clearly listed, and an agreement to pay was signed by you.

This is your final opportunity to pay the three past due installments and the current one. If payment of $420.00 is not received by September 22, 19_____, other actions will be taken to collect as deemed necessary.

We urge you to take action today.

Sincerely,

Dear Mr. Munson:

We are willing to allow you to make installment payments you can afford in order to pay your past due account of $1044.00.

Please call us today so we can agree on the payment amounts and dates.

It should be no surprise that this is our FINAL NOTICE. We have attempted unsuccessfully for over a year to obtain payment.

Our attorney will be notified to start collection procedures on January 17, 19__ unless we have come to a payment agreement before then. Please call or mail your check today.

Sincerely,

HELP DECLINED

Dear Mr. Sigrist:

You and we in the credit department have been unable to come to a mutually agreeable solution to your overdue account. You have declined all our suggestions for setting up a periodic payment plan. We cannot carry your account indefinitely.

Unless full payment of $521.40 is received by October 12, 19__, our only recourse is to pursue legal action.

The enclosed, postpaid envelope is for your convenience in mailing your check today.

Sincerely,

Dear Mr. Dukov:

We regret that our many efforts to reach an agreeable arrangement for paying your account have failed.

That being the case, we must make a more resolute attempt to collect your past due amount.

We expect to hear from you within ten days with a payment schedule or a check. If we do not, our attorney will be instructed to proceed with whatever action is required. Why not call now or mail your check today?

Sincerely,

DELINQUENCY REPORT

Dear Ms. Ramaker:

Although we do want our money right now, we are reluctant to call our collection agency and then report your delinquency to the Association Credit Bureau. That would make it more difficult for you to obtain credit elsewhere.

It is now up to you to stop us from making a delinquency report. You can do this by sending your check for the full $420.00 that is past due as soon as possible, but absolutely no later than October 3, 19__.

Sincerely,

Dear Mr. George:

As a member of the _____Retail Merchants Association, we are required to report past due customers. In our endeavor to keep your name off that report, we have sent you several letters requesting payment of your bill of $449.91.

We see one way for you to stay off the report, to retain your good credit record, and to avoid having your account turned over to the Collins

Collection Agency. That method is to pay your account before September 30, 19___.

The decision is yours.

Sincerely,

_____

Dear Mr. Kopplin:

Members of the Regional Credit Bureau report all long-overdue balances to the membership. Thus most local retailers have this information when you apply for credit.

We are sure you do not wish this to happen to you.

To maintain your current good credit standing, we must have a payment on your account by September 10, 19___. If we do not hear from you by that date, your account will be turned over to the collection department of the Regional Credit Bureau.

Please mail your check or get in touch with us today.

Sincerely,

_____

FIVE-DAY NOTICE

Dear Mr. Finley:

This FIVE-DAY NOTICE is the FINAL one we will send.

If your final billing of $171.20, copy enclosed, is not paid by September 6, 19___, we will refer your account to our Collection Department for whatever legal action they find necessary.

If you have any questions, please call our office at 000-000-0000. Even better, please mail your check today.

Sincerely,

_____

Dear Mrs. Hampton:

You have only FIVE DAYS in which to pay your gas bill. Our earlier reminders have not resulted in your paying the past due amount of $195.20.

To avoid our locking the incoming valve at the meter, we must have a payment by October 16, 19__.

Please respond immediately.

Sincerely,

SEVEN-DAY NOTICE

Dear Mr. Doyle:

SEVEN-DAY NOTICE

Your water service will be turned off without another notice if your bill of $74.00 is not paid within seven days—that is, on or before July 12, 19__.

If you have already made the payment, we thank you, and you may disregard this notice. If not, please mail your check today.

Sincerely,

Dear Mr. Herzog:

Payment of your $89.47 telephone bill may already have been made. If so we thank you.

If there is a reason for your delay, please call our customer service representative at 000-0000. We would welcome the opportunity to discuss a solution to your problem.

Unless we hear from you or receive payment by April 29, 19__, seven days from now, service will be discontinued.

Act promptly to avoid the cost and inconvenience of restoring your service. Mail your check today.

Sincerely,

FINAL APPEAL

Dear Mr. Bauman:

May we get serious for a moment? This is about your past due account, with a current balance of $696.53. Your last payment was received in May, and now it is November.

All our previous reminders, notices, letters, and phone calls have not succeeded in getting a payment from you.

We are now making our final appeal: Please mail your check for $696.53 by November 22. If we do not receive it by then, your account will be turned over to a collection agency. The resulting decline of your credit rating can be serious.

Mail your check no later than November 22 in the postage paid envelope enclosed.

Sincerely yours,

Dear Mr. Lewbel:

You will not hear from our attorney about your long-overdue account for another four days. The legal papers are ready, but we would appreciate hearing from you first. If we knew your problem, perhaps we could help.

If you are short of ready cash, we could work together on an installment plan. You probably have some ideas in mind. Let us hear them. You have only four days in which to call or make full payment.

Sincerely,

Dear Mr. Eldridge:

Our collections department has decided to start legal action to recover the $731.95 you have owed us for nearly two years. Our many reminders, letters and calls have brought no response from you.

I have persuaded the collections department to hold this action for another ten days. We fully appreciate the business you have given us, and we feel we can work out a payment agreement that will keep you out of court.

Please phone us today. We have only ten days.

Sincerely,

LAST CHANCE

Dear Mr. Olson:

You have made no payments on the $1391.10 in your overdue account.

Because you have not answered our previous correspondence and other attempts to contact you, our only recourse is to ask our attorney to proceed with legal action.

There is, however, one final chance for you to avoid the inconvenience and loss of credit standing that court action would cause: You can pay in full within ten days, no later than August 12, 19___.

Sincerely yours,

Dear Mr. Linstad:

You may have seen signs, as you approached a long stretch of road heading into the desert, that say, "Last Chance for Gas."

This is your "Last Chance to Pay" before we turn your account over to our attorney for collection.

You have been sent reminders and letters during the past year, but have made no apparent effort to pay your bill.

You may either pay in full or discuss a payment plan with us by November 12, 19___, ten days from now, or we will have our attorney pursue the collection of your account.

Please contact us before November 12.

Sincerely,

Dear Mr. Nierling:

All of our requests for payment of your past due $329.47 have been ignored.

We see no alternative to turning your account over to a collection agency if you do not pay or avail yourself of this final opportunity to work with us on a payment schedule. This must be done within ten days, by October 13, 19.

Enforced collection procedures can be costly and also impair your credit rating.

May we hear from you today?

Sincerely,

Dear Mrs. Sturner:

When you purchased your washer and dryer on March 10, 19___, the contract called for six equal monthly payments. It also stated that if payments were not made on time, the total balance owing became immediately due.

We have been more patient than required, and, as you know, you now have three payments past due. We therefore request payment in full.

We will expect payment within ten days from the date of this letter. If you have not responded by then, your account will be turned over to a collection agency or an attorney.

Your prompt action would be appreciated.

Sincerely,

FINAL NOTICE

Dear Mr. Baines:

FINAL NOTICE

We have a policy whereby past due accounts are to be turned over to the Bureau of Medical Business for collection.

Because your account is past due, we will be required to turn it over to the Bureau for collection unless payment is made within ten days from the date of this letter.

Sincerely,

WARNING

This is our FINAL NOTICE, __(customer name)__, regarding the total amount owing on your account. If we do not hear from you within fifteen days from the date of this letter, your account may be referred to a collection agency.

You don't want this to happen and we don't want to take this kind of drastic action. It's up to you.

Return your credit card and pay your account today.
    Minimum Payment Due $_____
    Total Amount Owing $_____

Sincerely,

    __(customer name)__
    __(Address)__
    __(Account number)__

Dear Mr. Goyer:

LAST NOTICE

The attached statement indicates an overdue balance of $2741.29, which was due in May of last year.

Because you have declined to make payments on this account or to provide us with an explanation for your delinquency, legal enforcement may be taken without further notice to you. Why not avoid this? Mail your check today.

Sincerely,

Dear Mr. Hendricks:

This is your FINAL NOTICE before our auditing firm closes your account.

Our last of many efforts to obtain payment will be to turn your account over to the Credit Bureau for collection. This will complicate further service from us and limit your credit with other firms.

To forestall this action, mail your check for $722.40 by January 30, 19__.
Remember, this is your final notice.

Sincerely yours,

Dear Mr. McClaron:

This is a FINAL NOTICE.

We have tried numerous times during the past year to resolve the problems related to your past due account, but with no success.

We will allow you another ten days, until July 21, 19__, to pay your account. If payment is not received during those ten days we will instruct our attorney to initiate collection procedures.

We believe it would be to your benefit to pay immediately. Mail your check today.

Sincerely,

Dear Mr. Jarrett:

FINAL NOTICE

Because you have not replied to our recent letters or paid your overdue account, we see no recourse but to place your account with our attorney for collection.

We have asked him to advise you on March 15, 19__ of the action he will take.

This gives you until March 13 to clear your account and not have to live through the embarrassment of legal enforcement.

Please take advantage of this final opportunity. Mail your check today.

Sincerely,

LETTERS TO ATTORNEY OR AGENCY

Dear Mr. Stockton:

Enclosed are our complete files for each of the persons listed below. **Please start collection procedures as soon as practicable.**

Name	Balance Due
	$

Sincerely,

Dear Ms. Webster:

Re: Mr. John C. Johnston
    (address)
    $_____ past due

We are sending you this account for collection.

Enclosed is our complete file of billings, payments and correspondence to and from Mr. Johnston covering the debt in question.

Please let us know if we can provide any other information.

Sincerely,

SKIP TRACING

Comments

A person may fail to notify his creditors of his new location either on purpose or by carelessness. He is a "skip." For you to collect he must be located. One of many location techniques is to write to a person or business that knew the debtor. His credit application is a good place to start.

Dear Mr. Farber:

We are attempting to locate Mr. Wilbur K. Mathews. We understand he previously resided at:
    0000 Main Street
    City, State, ZIP

We would appreciate your help in providing us with his present residence or business address. If not available, do you know of a friend or acquaintance of his we might contact?

Your reply will be greatly appreciated.

Sincerely,

Dear Mrs. Tracy:

You were mentioned on the credit application of Mrs. Bradford A. Malone of 0000 Center Avenue, Spring Valley, MN as a close relative. It is important that we contact her.

We would greatly appreciate your writing her present address at the bottom of this letter and mailing it in the postpaid envelope enclosed.

Sincerely,

CHAPTER *8*

Series of Collection Letters to Consumers

The fundamental belief behind all collection letters is that the customer will pay if reminded regularly and with successively increasing insistence.

One way to make the collection writing task easier is to prepare a series of letters. These can be organized ahead of time and varied as individual situations demand. The first one or two letters could be printed forms. After that, individually typed letters, even if typed from a master, are more effective.

Vary the series from time to time. A customer will lose his respect for you if he starts receiving the same series of reminders he got the last time his payments were slow.

Study the comparative effectiveness of your various series and attempt to determine if a four-letter series collects as well as a six-letter series. If four letters have not elicited a payment, more colorful attention-getting techniques can be used such as using colored paper. Buff is good and imparts a feeling of superior authority, but this color will soon become overused and lose its impact. However, any color that stands out from the mass of white letters and envelopes such as pink, yellow, green, orange, or red will draw attention to <u>your</u> letter.

CAPITALS, **bold print** and <u>double underlining</u> are attention getters when used sparingly. Overuse, however, dulls the reader's sensitivity to them.

HOW TO DO IT

1. Let the reader know this is a collection letter.
2. Mention one or more facts related to the particular situation.
3. Request prompt payment.

SERIES ONE, THREE LETTERS: PAST DUE CHARGE ACCOUNT

Letter One

Dear Mr. Moyer:

Satisfying your personal needs is our prime concern. We hope you value our trust and friendship as much.

Recently your account has become overdue. Several notices making you aware of this were mailed with your monthly statements. Once again, you are being asked for immediate payment of $87.50.

Serving you and your family still remains our first desire. Please call us or stop by the store so we may discuss the easiest way for you to meet this obligation.

Sincerely,

Letter Two

Dear Mr. Moyer:

Sending another notice about your unpaid account upsets us greatly. Your credit was accepted because you had proved you were a trustworthy customer.

Your trust with us can still be kept by paying the full amount of $87.50. Pay today and avoid jeopardizing your credit reputation.

Very truly yours,

Letter Three

Dear Mr. Moyer:

We are in business to serve our customers and cannot afford to spend too much time trying to collect the $87.50 you owe us. One week from the above date, we will turn your account over to our lawyer. We hope you prefer to make your payment to us rather than to have our lawyer contact you.

Yours truly,

SERIES TWO, THREE LETTERS: PAST DUE SUBSCRIPTION

Letter One

Dear Mr. Maguire:

It is easy to forget things in the rush of business. You dash to the office and leave your briefcase on the table, or you dash from your car and leave the keys in the ignition.

It may have slipped your mind that the payment for your subscription to _____ is past due.

A second bill and convenient envelope are enclosed for the check we hope you will mail today.

Sincerely,

Letter Two

Dear Mr. Maguire:

"Now what's wrong?" is a common question. May we ask you if anything is wrong with your subscription to _____, the magazine? the service? the whatever?

Please let us know and we will do everything in our power to set it straight.

If you have only put off your payment, please take care of it now. A duplicate invoice is enclosed.

Sincerely,

Letter Three

Dear Mr. Maguire:

You haved not responded to our inquiries about payment for your subscription to _____. The bill is long overdue, and it is casting a shadow on your credit rating, a precious asset you cannot ignore.

Another bill is enclosed. Unless payment is received by January 21, 19__, no further issues will be sent.

Sincerely,

SERIES THREE, THREE LETTERS: OBLIGATION TO PAY

Letter One

Dear Mr. Meline:

Perhaps you have overlooked the recent reminders we have sent regarding your overdue balance of $297.87.

Would you please mail your check today?

Sincerely,

Letter Two

Dear Mr. Meline:

We believe we fulfilled our obligation to you by shipping quality lumber at the time and place you requested. We, in turn, expect you to fulfill your obligation by paying for the merchandise.

If there is a problem with the lumber or difficulty in paying the $297.87 due us, please provide an explanation so we can work together toward a solution.

A payment today would be appreciated.

Sincerely,

Letter Three

Dear Mr. Meline:

Your balance owing of $297.87 is now 120 days past due.

We believe you should take all steps possible to uphold the value of your credit reputation. One step is to make a prompt payment.

If, however, we do not receive full payment by April 14, 19__, we will turn your account over to Local Collectors, a collection agency.

Sincerely,

SERIES FOUR, THREE LETTERS: REMINDERS

Letter One

Dear Ms. Holton,

Just a reminder . . .

of the amount at the bottom of this note. It hasn't been paid. Will you mail your check today? $94.80

Sincerely,

Letter Two

Dear Ms. Holton,

Has the mail been delayed again . . .

preventing your check from reaching us? Did you mail a payment on your account recently? If you did, please stop payment and send another check for $94.80. We are anxious to have your account on a current basis.

With hope,

Letter Three

Dear Ms. Holton,

There must be a reason . . .

why we haven't heard from you after our previous reminders.

Will you let us know why? Perhaps you have merely overlooked the due date, or perhaps you would like to spread the balance over a longer period. Please let us know how we can help, because your overdue account must be paid.

The amount due is $94.80.

Concerned,

SERIES FIVE, FOUR LETTERS: GARDEN TOOL PURCHASE

Letter One

Dear Mr. Avery:

Have you overlooked the statement we mailed to you on May 10, 19— covering gardening tools you purchased on April 29?

The amount due is $221.45.

Sincerely,

Letter Two

Dear Mr. Avery:

You have not responded to our previous reminders about your tool purchase in April. We realize that statements and letters get misplaced and forgotten, but your payment of $221.45 is overdue.

May we have your check today?

Sincerely,

Letter Three

Dear Mr. Avery:

Payment of your May 10, 19__ statement was due June 10, 19__. That was three months ago. We are sure you found our garden tools satisfactory since we have not heard otherwise.

I am also sure you believe in fairness to both supplier and customer. We ask that you now do your part by paying for the tools purchased.

The amount due is $221.45. Please mail your check today.

Sincerely,

Letter Four

Dear Mr. Avery:

You seem reluctant to pay us $221.45 for the garden tools you bought in April. We have had no response to our letters requesting payment.

Now we expect you to pay us within ten days from the date of this letter. If payment is not received by then, our only recourse is to turn your account over to a collection agency.

Very truly yours,

_____

SERIES SIX, FOUR LETTERS: CHARGE ACCOUNT

Letter One

_____

Dear Ms. Anthony:

We're reminding you that your account is now 20 days overdue.

Please disregard this notice if you have already mailed us your check for $196.05.

Cordially,

_____

Letter Two

_____

Dear Ms. Anthony:

We would like to continue our friendship while doing business with you. However, we need to have you send us a check for $196.05 to cover your overdue account. Please mail your check today.

Sincerely,

_____

Letter Three

_____

Dear Ms. Anthony:

We have not heard from you regarding your long-standing past due account of $196.05. This account has been overdue since _____.

You have been a reliable customer, and we would like to continue our friendly business relationship. Only if you pay your past due account can we continue to offer you our quality merchandise and helpful service.

Please let us know if you have a problem in paying this. Otherwise we expect you to pay the $196.05 today.

Sincerely,

Letter Four

Dear Mr. Anthony:

We still have not heard from you regarding your overdue balance of $196.05. If this account is not paid within ten days, we will turn it over to our attorney. Please mail your check today to prevent our starting this legal action.

Very truly yours,

SERIES SEVEN, FOUR LETTERS: BUSINESS APPRECIATED

Letter One

Dear Mr. Egland:

Just a friendly reminder that your account with us is now due.

A check today for $492.50 will keep your balance from becoming past due.

Swanson's appreciates your business.

Cordially,

Letter Two

___

Dear Mr. Egland:

Your payments have always been on time, except for your last purchase for $492.50.

We hope that this second reminder will prompt you to make a payment today.

Swanson's appreciates your business.

Sincerely,

___

Letter Three

___

Dear Mr. Egland:

Our previous letters have brought no reply from you.

At this time we must request that you make a payment on your long overdue account. As much as "Swanson's appreciates your business," we cannot continue to carry your account without some payment or word from you that explains your lack of action.

Only your immediate attention to this account will keep your credit rating intact, because reports of past due accounts are sent to the Retail Credit Association.

Please reply today with a payment of $492.50.

Sincerely,

___

Letter Four

___

Dear Mr. Egland:

Our slogan, "Swanson's appreciates your business," is a truism. Another truism is that Swanson's cannot disregard overdue account balances.

You have had ample opportunity to pay your balance of $492.50. This is our last letter to you. It is a final notice.

Unless payment is received within twelve days from the date of this letter, the collection department of the Retail Credit Association will be given your account for collection.

Sincerely,

SERIES EIGHT, FOUR LETTERS: PATIENCE

Letter One

Dear Mrs. Haas:

Just a reminder that your account is 15 days past due.

If you have already sent your check for $229.97, we thank you for doing so.

Cordially,

Letter Two

Dear Mrs. Haas:

Patience is a virtue. We may sometimes seem lacking because we get a little impatient, but we try to be considerate of our friends and customers. Please accept this letter in that spirit.

Your account has become long past due (since March 15). Please mail your check for $229.97 today. We are expecting it.

Sincerely,

Letter Three

Dear Mrs. Haas:

You have been a customer of ours since 19__, a long time. I am sure the reason is not only because we carry merchandise you like but because of our helpful clerks, our easy-pay credit policy, our prompt delivery service (at no extra charge), and our long-established reputation for quality.

We do all these things to please our customers and to cooperate with them. However, cooperation is a two-way street. By paying your bills on time, we have the funds to replenish our supplies and to continue providing helpful service to our customers.

Your account has remained unpaid since March 15. If you are unable to make full payment now, please call or write so we can make other arrangements with you. Otherwise, would you please help us to continue helping you by mailing your check for $229.97 today? A postpaid envelope is enclosed for your convenience.

Sincerely,

Letter Four

Dear Mrs. Haas:

Your response to our letters about your long-overdue account has been completely negative. Not one word has been heard from you.

We feel, therefore, that we must turn your account over to our attorney for collection. We dislike doing this, and in fairness to you we will postpone any action for ten days, giving you until June 27, 19__. Please mail us your check for $229.97 before that date to avoid the embarrassment of legal action.

Sincerely,

SERIES NINE, FOUR LETTERS: FAIRNESS

Letter One

Dear Mr. Breisler:

Just a reminder of your past due balance of $87.55. Perhaps in the rush of daily activities it has been overlooked.

Also, let us remind you of our annual Summer Sale that starts next month.

Sincerely,

Letter Two

Dear Mr. Breisler:

Forty-five days ago your account became overdue. We are puzzled. Have you still overlooked this bill?

We were prompt in delivering your order, and we think fairness suggests a prompt payment by you.

May we have your check today for $87.55? An envelope is enclosed for your convenience.

Sincerely,

Letter Three

Dear Mr. Breisler:

Our senior accountant asked me today when I expected you to clear your past due balance. I was surprised you had not yet responded to our previous notices and two letters.

If there is a problem, please explain on the back of this letter and mail it in the enclosed envelope. We will do what we can to help you retain your credit rating.

A check for $87.55 mailed today will save you the trouble of writing the letter.

Sincerely,

Letter Four

Dear Mr. Breisler:

We are at a loss to understand why you have apparently taken no action whatsoever to clear your account. It is now _____days past due.

Under these circumstances, we see no other course than to turn your account over to a collection agency. The agency will be notified in ten days unless your check for $87.55 is received today.

Sincerely,

SERIES TEN, FOUR LETTERS: FRIENDSHIP

Letter One

Dear Mrs. Schendel:

Just a note to let you know we appreciate having you for a customer. We realize that through an occasional oversight even our best customers may miss a payment.

A payment today will save you the 1½ percent monthly financial charge on your outstanding charge of $219.10.

If you have already paid, we send our thanks.

Sincerely,

Letter Two

Dear Mrs. Schendel:

Our records indicate your account is slightly past due. If we have been at fault in any way, please let us know so we may correct the error.

If there is no problem, a check today for $219.10 would be appreciated.

We strive to provide service with a friendly smile.

Sincerely,

Letter Three

Dear Mrs. Schendel:

We want every customer to be a friend. Part of our effort to accomplish this is to extend credit to our many customers. That, of course, assumes an obligation on your part to pay according to the terms agreed upon.

Right now, you are three months behind in your payments. The amount is $219.10.

The more letters we write to remind you of a past due account, the more fragile our friendship becomes.

We don't want to lose you as a friend. Please mail your check today for $219.10.

Sincerely,

Letter Four

Dear Mrs. Schendel:

We have been as lenient as we can and fear a strain in our friendship.

Your account of $219.10 is nearly five months past due, and we cannot continue to let it run any longer.

This is a final notice.

Unless specific arrangements that you can adhere to are made by May 12, 19___, your account will be turned over to our legal staff for collection.

Sincerely,

SERIES ELEVEN, FOUR LETTERS: COOPERATION

Letter One

Dear Mr. Liberko:

Your account at Swego Appliance Mart is a little past due. Could you see your way clear to mailing your payment of $129.40 today?

With thanks,

Letter Two

Dear Mr. Liberko:

Your account at Swego Appliance Mart is now 30 days past due.

We think you should mail a payment right away. How about today? The amount due is $129.40.

Regards,

Letter Three

Dear Mr. Liberko:

Swego Appliance Mart is still waiting for your payment of $129.40 to clear your overdue account.

We feel we have done our part by providing reliable merchandise at competitive prices and unequaled delivery service.

Your cooperation is now requested. You could mail your check today. Please do so before you put it off again.

Sincerely,

Letter Four

Dear Mr. Liberko:

Your reluctance to make payments on your overdue account at Swego Appliance Mart is a serious matter. Having been unsuccessful in getting you to pay for the merchandise you purchased, we must now take other steps.

Unless full payment of $129.40 is received by September 29, 19___, we will turn your account over to a collection agency.

You may save yourself the resulting embarrassment and loss of credit rating only by mailing us your check before then.

Very truly yours,

SERIES TWELVE, FOUR LETTERS: A PROBLEM?

Letter One

Dear Mr. Imhoff:

It is a pleasure having you as a customer, and we want to do everything possible to serve you well.

You opened your account with the understanding that payments would be made every thirty days. But we are surprised to learn that your account is now past due in the amount of $475.00.

May we have your cooperation in maintaining our good relationship by mailing us a check today?

Sincerely,

Letter Two

Dear Mr. Imhoff:

We know the ease with which a bill may be held aside or misfiled. Could that have happened to our statement of January 10, 19__?

If there is a reason for further delay of your payment of $475.00, please contact us. We will work with you.

Otherwise, a check for the minimum payment of $86.00 will be appreciated. Today, please.

Sincerely,

Letter Three

Dear Mr. Imhoff:

When a good customer gets behind in his payments, there must be a good reason. In our last letter, we asked you to contact us if you had a reason for further delay. We have heard nothing from you.

Do you have a question about the merchandise, the service, the terms of payment, or some other difficulty? Please let us know. We appreciate your business, and do not want to lose a good customer.

Your minimum payment is $86.00; the full amount is $475.00. Please get in touch or mail your check today.

Sincerely,

Letter Four

Dear Mr. Imhoff:

In business as well as in games, time limits are set. Our time limit for carrying your open account has been reached.

You have not communicated your reason for non-payment, and we do not know how to help you.

Unless we receive your check for full payment of $475.00 by July 20, 19__, our collection agency will start its collection procedures.

Very truly yours,

SERIES THIRTEEN, FOUR LETTERS: LOAN, PAST DUE

Letter One

Dear Mr. Tisdall:

May we call your attention to your loan payment that you have no doubt overlooked? It is thirty days past due. The amount is $260.32. Please mail your check today.

Sincerely,

Letter Two

Dear Mr. Tisdall:

Your loan payment is now forty-five days past due. Prompt payment of $260.32 would be appreciated. Please mail your check today.

Respectfully,

Letter Three

Dear Mr. Tisdall:

Again we call your attention to your loan payment due March 15. If there is some reason for the delay, please let us know.

We would appreciate receiving your check for $260.32 immediately.

Very truly yours,

Letter Four

Dear Mr. Tisdall:

It bothers us to have to say this, but we request that you pay the $260.32 owed to us. If we don't receive your check by November 31, we will be required to turn your account over to a collection agency.

Save yourself the embarrassment and loss of credit standing this would cause you. The enclosed envelope is for your payment. Please use it today.

Yours truly,

SERIES FOURTEEN, FOUR LETTERS: LOAN, CREDIT RATING

Letter One

Dear Mr. Spear:

This is just a reminder that your loan of $197.00 was due September 10, 19__.

Sincerely,

Letter Two

Dear Mr. Spear:

This is our second reminder that your loan of $197.00 was due September 10, 19__. Do not let your slow payments harm your credit rating any further.

Please mail your check for $197.00 today.

Sincerely,

Letter Three

Dear Mr. Spear:

We all get busy and forgetful at times. Partial payments, as we agreed when the loan was made, must be arranged with us in advance of the due date.

Your partial payment of $25.00 received October 11, 19__ is not satisfactory.

Please mail your check for $172.00 today, right now while you are considering it.

Sincerely,

Letter Four

Dear Mr. Spear:

FINAL NOTICE

Your loan balance of $172.00 is now three months past due.

You have stated no disagreement with the amount.

Payment must be received within ten days from the date of this letter to prevent legal action.

Very truly yours,

SERIES FIFTEEN, FOUR LETTERS: INSTALLMENT PAYMENTS

Letter One

Dear Ms. Dyer:

Thank you for your recent payment. Considering the amount due, we would appreciate regular installments, to be received here prior to the tenth of each month. The amount now due is $_____. Please mail your installment payment today.

Sincerely,

Letter Two

Dear Ms. Dyer:

We have received no reply to our recent statements. May we have **a** payment today?

The amount now due is $_____.

Sincerely,

Letter Three

Dear Ms. Dyer:

We have had no response to our last two letters. Won't you mail your check now—today?

If you are unable to pay regular monthly installments, please get in touch so we can make arrangements satisfactory to both of us.

The amount now due is $_____.

Sincerely,

Letter Four

Dear Ms. Dyer:

You have not acted upon our previous statements and letters. Your account has been past due since _____.

Therefore, unless payment is received within ten days from the above date, our collection agency will take over your account.

The amount now due is $_____.

Sincerely,

Comments

Five or six letters in a series is the most you should plan on. However, in the case of a long-time customer who is in temporary financial difficulties, or in a situation involving a close relationship between seller and buyer, more letters may be appropriate.

The number of letters in a series you mail to a particular customer should be varied, or the customer may wait until he knows the final letter has been sent before giving any consideration to paying.

SERIES SIXTEEN, FIVE LETTERS: INSTALLMENTS

Letter One

Dear Mr. Volden:

A friendly reminder that the first payment of $146.00 on your recent furniture installment contract was due five days ago.

If your check is in the mail, we send our sincere thanks. If not, please mail your check today.

Cordially,

Letter Two

Dear Mr. Volden:

This is our second reminder letter about a late payment on your purchase contract.

Please mail us a check today for $146.00.

Sincerely,

Letter Three

Dear Mr. Volden:

A third notice about the overdue payments on your furniture purchase contract is apparently necessary.

Is there a problem, either with the furniture or your ability to make monthly payments of $146.00? Please contact us by phone or letter or come in to our store to discuss this matter with us. You will find us fully cooperative with you in rewriting the contract if that will help you. Of course payment is always appreciated, so please mail your check today if you can.

Sincerely,

Letter Four

Dear Mr. Volden:

Is it possible that your circumstances have changed since we wrote your contract? Your credit at that time was sound, but we have received no payments. Your first payment is now forty-five days past due, and your second payment is fifteen days overdue.

A good credit rating is essential if you are to continue making credit purchases. Your payment record is available to all merchants of the

Fairview Retailer's Association. We expect a prompt payment of $292.00. Please mail it today.

Sincerely yours,

Letter Five

Dear Mr. Volden:

We were happy when you purchased a new dining room set from us, and you appeared pleased with the furniture. We arranged a contract for easy monthly payments which you agreed you could make on time.

Having received no payments or any indication of your interest in rescheduling payments, we have concluded that we can no longer carry your account.

This decision means that you will pay the full amount owed, $3504.00, no later than November 17, 19__, or our attorney will be instructed to arrange for collection of the amount due.

A payment today will relieve you of concern about legal action.

Respectfully,

SERIES SEVENTEEN, SIX LETTERS: LIMIT REACHED

Letter One

Dear Mr. Janus:

If you have already mailed your check for $333.47 for the items listed on our statement of July 10, 19__, you may disregard this notice.

If not, please use the enclosed, postpaid envelope to mail your check today.

Sincerely,

Letter Two

Dear Mr. Janus:

In the past you were punctual in making payments, and we feel we can rely on your high standard.

Prompt payments enable us to provide our customers with the best service. You can help us serve you better by mailing your check today. The amount is $333.47.

Sincerely,

Letter Three

Dear Mr. Janus:

We have written you twice requesting payment of your balance of $333.47. Is something wrong? If there is, please let us have a frank explanation. Then we can work together to arrive at a mutually satisfactory solution. Otherwise, please mail your check today.

Sincerely,

Letter Four

Dear Mr. Janus:

Because you have not replied to our previous letters, we now urge you to pay the balance of $333.47 in your account.

The fact that you have an open account is an indication of our confidence in your willingness to pay, but there is a limit to how long an account can go unpaid, and that limit has been reached.

Please confirm our confidence in you by writing your check today.

Sincerely,

Letter Five

Dear Mr. Janus:

We have received no response to our many letters requesting payment of your past due account of $333.47. Therefore, we feel we should place your account with a collection attorney.

This would result in embarrassment, expense, and loss of credit rating.

You can forestall our taking this action and retain our good opinion of your integrity by mailing your check today. We expect to receive your check within four days.

Sincerely,

Letter Six

Dear Mr. Janus:

As treasurer, I often review accounts that have been processed for handling by our collection attorney. Some customers are long-time friends, some have long records of on-time payments and some are new and not familiar with our policy of honesty and fairness.

Legal action is a burden to all involved, and we believe it should not be necessary in this case.

There must be a reason for your not paying your account of $333.47, perhaps a personal problem. Please use the enclosed envelope marked "confidential" to explain to me personally. We can work out something to help us both.

I will hold your account open for another ten days. Please reply before then.

Sincerely,

SERIES EIGHTEEN, SIX LETTERS: RESPONSIBILITY

Letter One

Dear Mr. Zell:

Only a reminder, Mr. Zell, that your account is overdue. The amount is $295.90. Please mail your check today.

Sincerely,

Letter Two

Dear Mr. Zell:

A reminder, in fact the second one, that you have an overdue amount of $295.90. May we hear from you soon? Why not mail your check today?

Sincerely,

Letter Three

Dear Mr. Zell:

Although you have neither paid your past due balance of $295.90 nor offered an explanation, we assume you intend to pay.

If you have a problem, you will have our full cooperation in solving it. Let us have a visit or letter or phone call or, even better, a check from you within five days.

Sincerely,

Letter Four

Dear Mr. Zell:

You are no doubt proud of your credit standing. You are able to purchase what you need when you need it. This convenience, however, carries a corresponding responsibility: to make payments within terms agreed upon when making a purchase.

Our terms have always been payment in full 30 days from the billing date. If you have a problem paying the full amount of $295.90, a partial payment of $100 will be acceptable.

Your cooperation by mailing a check today would be appreciated.

Sincerely,

Letter Five

Dear Mr. Zell:

Your goodwill is vitally important to us. That is why we are so concerned about your not paying even a part of the $295.90 you have owed us for a long time.

We wonder if you have lost interest in keeping your account on a current basis. That can result in our curtailing your future purchases. Because neither of us wants that, please mail your check today—right now would be a good time.

Sincerely,

Letter Six

Dear Mr. Zell:

Your long overdue account balance of $295.90 concerns us. We have offered patience, we have suggested a partial payment, and we have hinted at your losing further credit.

At this time we can carry you no longer. We must take action to obtain the money that is rightfully ours.

We will be patient, however, for another twelve days to allow you to arrange some means for payment. If we have not received your check by then, your account will be turned over to _____, a collection agency.

Sincerely,

COLLECTION AGENCY CONSUMER LETTERS

Comments

The two letters below advising the debtor to answer within 30 days applies to consumer purchases only. This is not required in commercial collection notices.

Dear Mr. Mitford:

This is our official notification that this account has been assigned to us for immediate collection. Please make payment in full now or present your defense against this claim within 30 days.

    To: Mr. H. W. Mitford
    Creditor: Jones Construction Co.
    Principal: $192.40   Interest: $1.48
    BALANCE DUE: $193.88

We believe you want to pay your just debts. If the amount shown is incorrect or not owed by you, send us a written notice within 30 days. We will obtain verification of the debt and the amount due and mail you a copy, along with the name and address of the original creditor if different from the one indicated.

If you do not notify us in writing within 30 days we will assume the amount due is correct.

The full amount due must be paid to clear your account.

Sincerely,

Dear Mr. Sorrell:

Your account has been placed with us for immediate collection. You owe the total amount of $499.95 to Windfall Equipment Co.

Because credit is one of your most precious possessions, protect it by paying now. We must have payment within five days from the date of this letter.

If you notify this office within 30 days of receiving this notice that you dispute the validity of the debt or any portion thereof, this office will obtain verification of the debt or obtain a copy of the judgment against you and mail you a copy of such judgment or verification.

If you request in writing within 30 days after receiving this notice, this office will provide you with the name and address of the original creditor, if different from the current creditor.

Yours sincerely,

_____

Part **III**

BUSINESS TO BUSINESS LETTERS

CHAPTER 9

Credit Letters, Business to Business

Business credit letters include subjects from granting credit to canceling credit, from providing a credit reference to explaining cash discounts, from thanking a customer for his first order to requesting a personal guaranty.

A letter to a large organization must clearly identify the situation or problem because you don't know for sure who will answer your letter.

Because future sales and profits depend on the goodwill of your customers, your letters must not antagonize. No matter how insistently you refuse credit or how wrong your customer is, goodwill demands politeness and consideration for your buyer's point of view.

HOW TO DO IT

1. State the reason for your letter in the first sentence.
2. Clarify the situation or problem.
3. Suggest a solution.
4 Ask for the reader's cooperation.

WELCOMING NEW CUSTOMERS

Comments

A welcome letter to a new or former customer is a letter of happiness and sincerity. Make the reader glad he asked for credit from you. This is a great opportunity to do a little promotional work for your company and your products.

Terms of sale can be formalized by including them in your welcoming letter.

Dear Mr. Pierce:

We would like to take this opportunity to welcome you as one of Compower's customers and acquaint you with our practices.

Compower is a company that prides itself on its unique and custom products. Our engineering department is highly skilled and intensely involved in producing a power supply to meet your individual needs. Our engineers work closely with you to customize a power supply that meets your exact specifications. We use high quality components and have engineering specialists to manufacture custom parts unique to your power supply.

Compower's financial terms are net of invoice at 30 days. Our prices are based on receiving payment within these terms. Your assistance in maintaining a current balance will be greatly appreciated.

To assist Compower in establishing a credit line for your company, we have enclosed an application for credit. Should you have any questions concerning the credit application, please feel free to contact me at any time.

Sincerely,

Dear Mr. Noe:

A line of credit has been opened for you. Welcome aboard! We are happy to have you join us and will do all we can to make our relationship pleasant— and also profitable for you.

The quality of our door hardware and locks is assured because we carry only the top line. Our competitive edge is our rapid delivery service. We guarantee the best service because we have our own fleet or delivery trucks and maintain the largest inventory west of Chicago. All orders are filled the day received, and when possible we deliver the same day.

Our terms are 1% ten days, net 30 days.

We look forward to helping you.

Cordially,

Dear Mr. Raft:

It is always a pleasure to welcome a new customer by extending both the hand of friendship and a line of credit.

We understand you are new in this area but were well established in __(city)__. If we can be of assistance in helping you get acquainted in our community, please let our salesman, Mr. Dave Watkins, know. He likes to expound his knowledge of local people and businesses.

Our terms are 1% 30 days, net 31, and your credit is open, subject to review in three months.

Again, welcome.

Cordially,

Dear Mr. Goode:

It is good to hear from a former customer, and we thank you for your order No. 1444 of July 21, 19__.

We will be willing to grant credit again on our regular terms of 1% 30 days, net 31 days, <u>provided that</u> you clear an old balance of $219.40. This balance relates to your order No. 722 of February last year.

When this overdue amount is paid we will process your current order.

Sincerely,

Dear Mr. Fernald:

Although we have not done business with each other for over a year, we believe both companies would benefit if we offered you payment-with-order terms or C.O.D. shipments. That would enable you to continue carrying our highly recognized lines.

I'll have our sales department call you next week to discuss this, and we will look forward to seeing an order from you then.

Sincerely,

Dear Mr. Beckwith:

Welcome home! That may be a little strong, but it expresses our feelings.

We thank you for your order of May 12, 19__. It has been a long time since your previous order, and we hope the next interval will be shorter. You can expect the same service we provided before, and a few lines have been added to our stock.

Our terms remain 1%, 15 days, net 30. When we receive a current financial statement, we will establish a line of credit so you may obtain merchandise quickly.

Sincerely,

CREDIT POLICIES EXPLAINED

Comments

Even if known in a general way, the details of your credit policies will not be familiar to your new credit customers. Also, credit policies change and need clarification.

In both cases, a letter relating your credit practices and expectations to your customers is a step toward continued or improved customer relations.

Dear Mr. Rogers:

Enclosed with this letter is a copy of our credit policies. We hope that the written formalization of these policies will help avoid confusion between us and will clarify any questions you might have regarding our credit policies.

We consider adherence to these policies and a complete and current credit file on the customers to whom we extend credit an important part of our ability to continue to extend credit.

Therefore, please read over our policies carefully, complete the enclosed credit application/update, and return it to our office as soon as possible.

Please note we have provided a personal guaranty form. This is <u>not</u> requested or required from customers who maintain current balances. However, if your account is overdue, please include the personal guaranty.

If you have any questions regarding our policies or would like to discuss special arrangements, please get in touch with us.

Sincerely,

Comments

The individual guaranty form below is a standard form. A joint personal guaranty is nearly the same except that the names of both spouses are entered.

INDIVIDUAL PERSONAL GUARANTY

Date _____19__

I, __(name)__, residing at __(address)__, for and in consideration of your extending credit at my request to __(name of company)__, (hereinafter referred to as the Company), of which I am __(title)__, hereby personally guarantee to you the payment at __(address and city of creditor)__ in the State of __(State)__ of any obligation of the Company, and I hereby agree to bind myself to pay you on demand any sum which may become due to you by the Company whenever the Company shall fail to pay the same. It is understood that this guaranty shall be a continuing and irrevocable guaranty and indemnity for such indebtedness of the Company. I do hereby waive notice of default, non-payment and notice thereof and consent to any modification or renewal of the credit agreement hereby guaranteed.

Signature_____
Witness:_____
Address:_____

Dear Mr. McKay:

This is a general statement of our credit policy. Klein Products, Inc. will extend credit to its regular customers who desire credit and who have demonstrated an ability and willingness to pay their account within the Company's stated terms.

Customers who accept credit will be expected to maintain their accounts within the terms agreed upon.

We will sell new customers on a C.O.D. basis until proper credit worthiness is established. Part of establishing credit worthiness includes completion of our application form and our checking your references.

All existing customer accounts are assigned a Klein Products, Inc. letter as follows:

-A- "A" accounts are those that customers consistently maintain within the terms set forth by the Company. This includes customers who voluntarily pay cash, those who take cash discounts within the ten-day period prescribed, and those who pay net balances within thirty days.

"A" accounts are considered preferred, and the customers will be given preferential treatment by Klein Products, Inc. In addition, they will receive notice of all specials and all extra discount programs.

-B- "B" accounts are those that are occasionally paid late but are generally maintained within the prescribed terms and have never required collection agency action to cover past due balances.

"B" account customers will normally be given the opportunity to participate in all specials or extra discount programs.

-C- "C" accounts are those that are habitually paid late or have required some form of collection action to recover past due balances.

"C" account customers will generally be sold on a C.O.D. basis only.

Customers in the "C" category who bring their balances within the Company's terms and maintain them for at least 90 days will automatically be converted to the next higher classification and be accorded the additional privileges of the next classification.

Credit limits will be established on an account-by-account basis, and we will notify each customer of this limit. Typically, this will be an amount approximately equal to one month's average sales. With new customers, the limit will automatically be set at $1,000 until an appropriate credit record is established. Customers who exceed their credit limits or who become slow in payment of past due balances will be contacted first by mail and then by telephone to try to establish a program for maintaining a good credit record.

Service charges of 1.5% per month will be added to all accounts that consistently have past due balances. No service charge will be made on current accounts and no charge will be made if payments fall slightly behind on an occasional basis.

Continuing to accept credit from Klein Products, Inc. constitutes an agreement to pay these charges if and when it becomes necessary to assess them.

If your business is new and you cannot provide adequate references or your account is overdue and includes a history of slow payment, a personal guarantee is required.

If you have special requirements or unusual circumstances that require different terms, please contact us to discuss them. If it is mutually advantageous, we will do everything possible to accommodate you.

Best regards,

GRANTING CREDIT

Comments

Tell your reader the good news that he has been granted credit in the first sentence. A happy customer is a buying customer.

Your terms of sale should be explained in detail. The terms are now in writing; therefore, make sure they are accurate and complete.

A sentence or two about your product or service is appropriate, and you should end with an offer to be helpful to your new credit customer.

Dear Mr. Karnz:

Welcome to our growing number of credit customers. Your first order for 300 electric power drills has been accepted. You will also receive our guarantee of fast service, quality merchandise, and complete satisfaction.

Our credit terms are 2% 10 days, net 30 days, F.O.B. our factory. Our invoices are dated the day of shipment, and the 2% discount period starts with the invoice date rather than from the date of your receipt of the goods. A late payment charge of 1% per month is added to invoices not paid within the 30-day period.

We in the credit department look forward to a pleasant relationship with Giant Hardware and will be glad to answer any questions you may have.

Sincerely,

Dear Mr. Holmes:

Thank you for your initial order dated May 6, 19__. New customers are most welcome.

We have arranged a credit line of $5,000 as you requested.

Invoices are dated and mailed the day following shipment, and they are due in 30 days. Late charges of 1% per month are added after the 30-day period to the amount you owe.

Most of our customers avoid the extra charge by paying within the 30-day period.

Sincerely,

Dear Mr. Sommers:

Thank you for your order of June 15, 19__, placed through our representative, Mr. John Shanks. You will be glad to know your credit has been approved. Shipment will be made within five days on our regular terms of 1% 10 days net 30.

Our invoices are dated the day of shipment. We can both benefit by your taking advantage of our 1% discount when you pay within ten days.

We welcome you as a new customer and are always ready to be of service to you.

Sincerely,

Dear Mr. Ahern:

Your application for credit has been approved. It is a pleasure to welcome you to our growing group of customers.

Orders for in-stock goods are shipped the following day. For items not in stock, we will give you an estimated delivery date.

Invoices are sent with each order and are payable within 30 days. Our low prices preclude any discounts. Monthly statements are mailed only upon request.

Our salesman, Sam Johnson, will call on you at regular intervals, and between calls you can leave a message for him by calling 000-0000.

We look forward to a mutually beneficial business relationship. Again, welcome.

Sincerely,

_____

Dear Mrs. Lind:

Congratulations on having qualified for a line of credit. You no longer need to buy on cash or C.O.D. terms. Our credit terms are 1% 30 days net 31 days with late charges of 1% per month added after 60 days.

Your credit limit is $_____.

Continue to send us semi-annual statements, and we will increase your credit line as soon as conditions warrant.

Sincerely,

_____

CREDIT LINE INCREASE

Dear Mr. Sutton:

Your personal good standing with us qualifies your business for an increase in your credit line to $6,000. We know you will find this an added convenience in meeting your purchasing needs for the upcoming holiday season.

We value your business and look forward to serving your merchandise requirements.

Sincerely,

_____

Dear Mr. Thorson:

Congratulations on having earned an increase in your open line of credit. Your limit has been raised to $27,000.

Your consistently prompt payments and steady purchases have allowed us to help you this way. We wish you continued success in your business and realize that we both can prosper by continued cooperation.

Cordially,

TERMS EXPLAINED

Comments

As well as explaining your terms of sale to new customers, other problems relating to terms must be solved. These can include offering installment payments to slow payers, imposing late payment charges, unearned discounts taken, and requests for special terms.

You must determine how much you will bend to the wishes of your customers and how much you will hold to your stated terms. In either case, explain your decision as clearly as possible, keeping in mind that the source of your income is your customers.

Dear Mr. Walters:

In the past, we have sent out three reminder letters to customers before handing over debts to a collection agency. These procedures are costing an ever-increasing amount of money in terms of printing, stationery, postage, clerical, and interest costs. It has been decided, therefore, to revise these procedures starting ___(date)___ . As a valued customer you are being provided with advance notice of these changes.

Under the new system, a brief reminder of overdue accounts will be attached to all statements sent out one month after the end of the month of invoice. If no response is received, a final notice will be sent out 14 days later asking for payment within seven days. In the absence of a satisfactory reply, the debt will be turned over to our collection agency.

We regret the need to take this action, but we must point out that all credit customers have accepted our credit terms which state that payment will be made before the end of the month following the date of the invoice. We hope, therefore, that you will make a sincere effort to comply with our terms of sale.

Sincerely,

Dear Mr. Powell:

For many months you have been making payments several weeks after the due date. You appear to be paying invoices in batches rather than individually within our terms.

Perhaps we have not been clear in stating our terms. Let me explain them now.

Your credit terms are "1% 30 days," meaning that your checks must be in our office within 30 days from the invoice date to allow you to take the 1% discount.

If you prefer to continue paying several invoices at one time, we can change your terms to "1% 15 Prox," in which case payment is due here on the 15th of the month following the date of your invoice. If, however, the total amount of these invoices exceeds your credit limit of $26,000, more frequent payments will be necessary.

If you have any questions or wish to change your terms to "1% 15 Prox," please call me at 000-000-0000. I will be happy to discuss this with you.

Sincerely,

Dear Mr. Palmer:

We have noticed over the past year that you take advantage of our 2% 10 days discount only on rare occasions. Also, many of your invoices are paid long after our 30 day net period, thus incurring our 1½% per month late payment charge.

Paying so many invoices late does not enhance your credit standing with other suppliers when they ask us for your payment record.

If we could receive on-time payments on a regular basis our operations could be better scheduled and therefore more efficient. This would allow us to pass the savings on to you.

I believe we can work together to arrange an extended terms program. Please give me a call so we can discuss this possibility. It would help us both.

Sincerely,

Dear Mr. Cofman:

This letter is to confirm the sales terms we agreed to in our meeting yesterday.

"A" units purchased in a calendar month:
> Less than 10M (thousand): net 30 days.
> 10 M through 50M: 1% 30 days net 31 days.
> Over 50M: 2% 30 days net 31 days.

"B" units purchased in a calendar month:
> Through 50M: 1% 30 days net 31 days.
> Over 50M: 1% 60 days net 61 days.

A 1% per month late charge is added to all past due accounts.

    I believe this covers our conclusions, and we anticipate a continued pleasant relationship with you.

Regards,

TERMS, INSTALLMENTS

Dear Mr. Weld:

I want to thank you for your cooperation and hospitality during my visit to your plant yesterday. I believe we've satisfactorily resolved the issue of the $_____ balance in your account, and this letter will serve as confirmation of our agreement.

1. Your check No. 1744 of June 20, 19__ has already been applied against invoice No. B-47229 and invoice Nos. B-48110, B-48112, B-48114, B-48115, B-48116 and B-48119.

2. The remaining $_____ will be paid in equal principal installments of $_____ on the first of each month starting July 1, 19__ through the final payment of March 1, 19__.

3. This agreement will carry an annual interest rate of ____%, paid on the declining balance as each installment is paid.

4. In the event of failure to meet any installment on the due date (a) the full amount of the balance becomes due and payable, and (b) open account privileges, described below, will be immediately terminated.

5. In the meantime, we will continue credit account shipments up to a limit of $_____ outstanding at any time, provided invoices are paid within our normal selling terms.

To the best of my recollection, the above covers the full range and content of our discussion. I'm enclosing two copies, one for you to sign and return to me, the other for your file.

Again, my thanks for your valuable assistance in structuring this agreement.

Sincerely,

_____

Dear Mr. Heston:

Yes, we can arrange installment payments for your purchase of a specialized tank hauling truck. Because of the amount of individualized work required, we will need a one-fourth payment before we begin work.

At the time of delivery, we will require another one-fourth payment. Thereafter we can extend the installments for a full year with regular monthly payments. If these payments should not be made on time, the remaining balance will become immediately due and payable.

We hope this arrangement is agreeable to you. When the final decision to purchase is made, we will write a contract that includes the specific amounts and dates.

Thank you for this opportunity to explain our installment terms.

Sincerely,

_____

Dear Mr. Hippner:

Thank you for your letter explaining your difficulty in making payments and your suggestion for installment payments.

We understand your problem, but we try to avoid the practice of accepting extended installments. However, we will in this one instance make an exception to help you regain your financial balance.

We will accept your proposal of _____ monthly payments of $_____ starting February 10, 19__ plus interest at an annual rate of _____ percent computed monthly on the unpaid balance. If any payment is not received by the 10th of the month due, the total unpaid balance will become due immediately.

Please sign and date the statement below and return a copy of this letter to us in the enclosed envelope.

Sincerely,

I agree to the terms stated above.

_____   _____
(signature   (date)

Dear Mr. Johnson:

Thank you for your check of January 3, 19__ in the amount of $560.50. This accounts for all of your past due invoices.

However, you omitted the interest charges. As we have previously explained, it has long been our policy to add a service charge of 1% per month to all overdue balances.

We are enclosing a statement explaining how we arrived at service charges of $34.06. We would appreciate your prompt payment of this amount.

Sincerely,

Dear Mr. Follette:

Due to the high cost of carrying credit, we regretfully must begin charging for accounts unpaid within thirty (30) days of service rendered.

Charges incurred on or after ___(date)___ will be subject to a 1.5% monthly carrying charge (with a $1.00 minimum).

No charge will be made for accounts paid within thirty (30) days of service rendered.

It will be company policy to encourage payment at the time service is provided. When truly necessary, we will attempt to accommodate those with limited income or large orders. Your understanding will be greatly appreciated.

I wish to thank you for your past and future business. We shall always be here to serve your needs.

Sincerely,

Dear Customer:

Late charges cost everyone money. It costs us because of the additional paper work and processing time. It costs you because the cost of the extra work must be included in the prices of our products.

To be fair to our customers who pay on time, effective February 1, 19___, our bills will reflect a late payment charge.

That charge will be 1.5% on the unpaid balance at the end of each billing period. This is an annual percentage rate of 18%. Payments not received by the next month's billing date will be treated as late payments.

We believe this is fair to our prompt paying customers and hope it will encourage you to make each payment before the next billing date.

Sincerely,

Dear Mr. Orrie:

Thank you for your check dated April 2, 19___. It includes all your past due invoices.

You did, however, forget to include financial charges for the late payments. Our policy is to add 1% per month to all late payments. The enclosed statement lists each invoice you paid and the late charges you owe on each one.

Please send us a check for $197.34 today.

Sincerely,

TERMS, UNEARNED DISCOUNTS

Dear Mr. Sorensen:

Thank you for your check of June 19, 19___ for $402.50.

We are sorry, but the cash discount you deducted isn't in order. Under our terms of 1% days net 30, your discount period ended June 11, 19___.

Please send us another check for $4.07.

Sincerely,

Dear Ms. Barner:

We are pleased that Boston Supply Co. is again taking advantage of our cash discounts.

Probably through an oversight, the deductions taken with your last payment were more than you earned.

We have enclosed a listing of each invoice paid and the appropriate discount for each. You may include the $29.47 due with your next payment of invoices. Please list the $29.47 as "prior unearned discounts."

We appreciate your prompt payments.

Sincerely,

Dear Mr. Trombino:

Perhaps we did not explain our terms clearly when you first opened your account.

Our terms are 2% 10 days net 25. To receive the 2% discount our invoices must be paid within ten days from the invoice date.

Your check dated June 12, 19___ was after the discount period.

We trust our terms are clear now and hope you will take advantage of the discount.

We look forward to your next order, and meanwhile would appreciate receiving a check for $47.51.

Sincerely,

Dear Mr. Haggard:

Your check has been received in payment of our invoices 4722, 4723, 6811, and 6990. We thank you.

The discounts of $_____ and $_____ taken on the first two were unearned because the discount period had passed. In the past you had consistently paid within the discount period, and we will, this time only, consider your taking those discounts as an unintended error and accept your check as full payment.

We are sure you will be fair to our other customers and in the future take discounts only when earned.

We appreciate your continuing business.

Sincerely,

SPECIAL TERMS DENIED

Dear Mr. Hosler:

We fully appreciate your request for cash discounts for paying earlier than required by our terms of net 30 days.

Our prices are competitive within the industry and many are lower. We can do this because all possible cost savings are passed on to our customers, and cash discounts become an added cost of doing business. We feel there is no gain by increasing prices in order to allow discounts.

That is the reason we cannot grant your request for cash discounts.

We appreciate your frequent orders.

Sincerely,

Dear Mr. Agnew:

We are enclosing a copy of your purchase order No. 7772 dated July 14, 19__. In the terms box you have typed, "1% 10 days, net 30." Our terms are net 30 days.

Please issue another purchase order with terms noted as, "net 30 days" and mark the order "Replacing P. O. No. 7772" or some similar notation.

There may have been an error in entering the terms. Our terms have not changed in several years and are common in our industry.

Thank you for taking the time to revise your order, and we will start on it promptly.

Sincerely,

Dear Mr. Rowland:

Thank you for your order No. A-1742 of July 11, 19__, for which you have requested an August 1 billing date. As you know, our billing date is one day after the shipping date.

We can, however, bill you on August 1 if we hold the shipment until July 31. Therefore we will ship July 31 unless we hear otherwise.

We hope this meets with your approval.

Sincerely,

FINANCIAL DATA REQUESTED

Comments

When you ask a person or business to supply credit data upon which you can base a decision to grant or deny credit, you are writing an inquiry letter that should be made easy to answer. We recommend a form with items to check off or short blanks to fill in.

The questions you ask will vary considerably depending upon the information needed in a particular situation. Chapter 1 lists twenty-three possible questions.

Because the information available at companies you question can vary from detailed records to skimpy estimates, persistence may be required.

Dear Mr. Barring:

Thank you for your order of April 12, 19__. We appreciate your wanting to buy from us once again.

If you will send us a current financial statement, we will review your account and extend a line of credit if we possibly can.

A standard financial form is enclosed if you wish to use it. A return envelope is also enclosed.

Sincerely,

Dear Ms. Wallington:

Thank you for your inquiry about opening an account with Beemer, Inc.

We'll need some financial information from you. Please mail us your current financial statements or fill in the enclosed standard form. This information will be held in strict confidence and be used for credit purposes only.

Your prompt response would be appreciated, and we look forward to a relationship profitable to us both.

Sincerely,

Dear Mr. Carson:

We're presently reviewing your credit and order limits to better serve your current needs.

To do this, we'll need some financial information from you:

1. Your latest financial statements, or
2. The enclosed form filled in by you.

This information will be available only to our credit department to reevaluate the extent of your credit.

Your prompt action in providing this information will assure our prompt handling of your future orders.

Sincerely,

Gentlemen:

We have the name of your organization as a credit reference for:
___(firm name)___
___(address)___

It would be appreciated if you would give us the benefit of your credit experience with this company, as well as any other comments concerning its management and general reputation, which would assist us in extending an appropriate line of credit.

The information you share with us will be held in strict confidence and will be used for credit purposes only. We will welcome an opportunity to reciprocate at any time.

Year of first sale_____

Highest credit, last 12 months_____

Amount owing now_____

Amount past due_____

Terms of sale_____

Promptness in paying_____

Special comments_____

Enclosed for your convenience is a self-addressed envelope. Your early reply would be appreciated.

Cordially yours,

Gentlemen:

___(company name)___
___(address)___

Would you please submit the following credit information on the above-mentioned firm? We appreciate your cooperation and will gladly reciprocate any time.

___(list only___
___information___
___you need)___

Sincerely,

Dear Morrisy:

Your help in supplying the following information would be appreciated. It will help us to intelligently consider the advisability of opening an account for the below-named customer. The information received will be held in strict confidence.

Thank you,

Bank Reference Report

Customer name_____

Customer address_____

Customer account No._____

No. years with bank _____   No. years credit avail._____

Size balance kept _____   Size bank line _____

Any NSF's _____   Amt. line owing _____

Terms/security for accounts _____

Type loan (SBA, equip., personal, other) _____

Additional bank comments _____

_____

_____

Attention Credit Manager:

    Reference: __(customer name)__

                  __(address)__

Gentlemen:

Your firm's name has been supplied to us as a source of reference by the above-named customer.

To aid us in establishing an appropriate line of credit for this account, would you please complete the lower portion of this letter and return it in the enclosed envelope? Please be assured that this information will be held in the strictest confidence.

We appreciate your cooperation and hope that you will not hesitate to contact us should we ever be able to extend a similar service.

Sincerely yours,

Experience	Manner of Payment
Sold from_____	Prompt & Satisfactory____
Highest credit_____	Days slow_____
Terms_____	Slow & unsatisfactory____
Owing_____ Past due_____	Slow but collectible_____
Comments_____	Amount secured_____

_____

Dear Mr. Simms:

Your bank has been given to us as a reference by Mr. Seward of the Bell Iron Works. We are establishing a line of credit for them. Their first order is estimated at $4,500, with succeeding orders up to about $6,000.

Your help in providing financial and character data you have available would be greatly appreciated and held in confidence. You can count on us for reciprocal information about your clients.

Your prompt reply would be appreciated.

A postpaid envelope is enclosed for your convenience.

Sincerely,

Attn: Records Research Section

Dear Mr. Martel:

Regarding __(company)__ of __(address)__ , please confirm any liens, assignments, or encumbrances that currently exist.

Can we expect this information within two weeks?

Sincerely,

CREDIT APPLICATIONS

Dear Ms. Valdez:

We have noted a company name change from Californis Warehouse to Calendar Corporation. We attempt to make transitions of this nature as little an inconvenience as possible by honoring your first order to allow you to comply with our request to complete a new credit application.

Please note that this is not meant to be taken as a reflection of your credit rating with our firm. It is a required formality in order for us to continue extension of credit to your company.

I have attached a credit application which should be returned prior to the date of your next order. If I may be of assistance in this matter, please feel free to contact me.

Sincerely,

Dear Mr. Ridley:

I appreciate your cooperation in returning the completed credit application and am pleased to extend La Rhonde Construction credit on our terms of 2% 10, net 30 days.

I was glad to receive the information about your company sent to us by the Construction Association. They are, however, organized to provide primarily delinquent references.

Thanks again for your full cooperation. I look forward to a mutually beneficial relationship.

Sincerely,

Dear Mr. Winslow:

Thank you for your order No. CR2788 of September 20, 19__. It has been forwarded to the production department for shipment as requested on your order.

We find we need additional information to complete your credit application. Could you please mail us the data listed below this week:
Current financial statements.
A statement of your insurance coverages:
Casualty.
Business interruption.
Liability.
Four recent trade references.

Your cooperation is appreciated.

Sincerely,

GENERAL CREDIT INFORMATION REQUESTED

Dear Mr. Kearney:

Mr. Layton of Busbee Automotive has referred us to you for background data about that company. We are considering becoming a new supplier for Busbee.

Information about how the owners have handled their finances, their promptness in handling bills and business problems, and general impressions of their character will be greatly appreciated.

Your comments will be held in strict confidence.

Sincerely,

Dear Mr. Sambot:

Mr. Jakoby has suggested that you could provide us with some general information about his credit status.

Any information you can offer relating to his finances and character will be appreciated and kept confidential.

The enclosed envelope is for your convenience.

Sincerely,

CREDIT LIMITED, NEW OPERATIONS

Dear Mr. Rogers:

We appreciate receiving your order of January 20 for 50,000 boxes.

Because you have been in business only since October, we have not been able to obtain your financial and credit data through our normal sources. The pro-forma financial statements for your first year of operation are well presented. However, until we can compare those estimates with your actual performance, we would suggest splitting the order into three approximately equal parts. Each third would be paid for within our usual terms of 1% 30 days net 31 days. If you can pay earlier, we can ship the next third that much sooner.

We hope this temporary arrangement is agreeable with you. We look forward to helping you build your new business.

Sincerely,

Dear Mr. Cresswell:

Thank you for your order No. B-7721 dated April 29, 19___. We appreciate your interest in our company.

We are aware that your operation is new and that you are working hard to expand it. We will help as much as we can. Your recent financial statements, however, do not support an order as large as this one.

If you can reduce the size of your order by about half or pay half before we schedule production, we will be happy to start on it immediately.

We look forward to hearing from you in a couple days.

Sincerely,

Dear Mr. Crombie:

It is our pleasure to announce that your application for credit has been approved, with a limit of $_____.

Our terms are 1% 10 days net 30 days. Late charges of 1% per month are added to amounts not received within 30 days.

Because we have no prior credit history with you, the limit we have set is tentative. We will review your credit performance periodically and change your limit as warranted.

We look forward to a long business relationship with you.

Sincerely,

Dear Mr. Shubel:

Based on your credit application, which indicates your business is just starting, we can offer only limited credit. Your prospects appear excellent, but we must base our credit limits primarily on performance.

We will start with a limit of $500.00. Our terms are net 30 days, and we can allow no exceptions to the limit or payment period. Your credit may be increased as you prove your stability.

We wish you good fortune and a long association with us.

Sincerely,

Dear Mr. Busch:

Thank you for your order dated August 22, 19__. A study of your credit history indicates that the credit we offer must be limited. To start, we will fill your order and expect payment within our terms of 1% 30 days net 31 days. However, as soon as one order is paid for we will accept your next one.

As your credit situation improves we will be able to loosen these rather strict limitations.

We look forward to your continuing business.

Sincerely,

CREDIT REFUSED, LIMITED DATA

Comments

Refusing credit while not losing the customer can be a difficult and delicate task—but not formidable. Start with a positive statement about something you and your reader agree on or with a thank you for being interested in your firm. You can't duck the reason for your refusal, so state it in plain language. With this build up, say you can't offer credit at this time. This leaves the door open for cash purchases now and perhaps credit at a later date. Ask your reader to get in touch later and wish him well.

A detailed explanation of how to write a considerate and effective refusal letter can be found in the first section of Chapter 1.

Dear Mr. Wells:

We would sincerely like to establish an open line of credit for you, but at present we are not able to do so because of the limited information we have been able to obtain.

Perhaps you could send us a current financial statement, to be held in complete confidence, and the names of a few of your present suppliers. We can then reconsider our decision.

In the meantime, our excellent service and quality products are available to you on a cash-in-advance basis.

Let us hear from you soon.

Sincerely,

Dear Ms. Kannelbach:

Thank you for your order received yesterday. Former customers are most welcome.

We do, however, need current financial data: recent financial statements and name and branch of your present bank.

Please provide these as soon as possible so we can start working together again.

Sincerely,

Dear Mr. Truesdale:

Your request for an open line of credit has been received. We thank you for your interest in our company.

To consider granting credit, we will need some information from you. Could you send us:

1. Your latest financial statements.
2. The name of your bank.
3. The name of three or more companies from which you are now buying.

We will get in touch with you as soon as we review this information.

Sincerely,

Dear Mr. Meza:

We appreciate your interest in our lines of quality self-propelled yard-maintenance equipment.

As much as we want new customers and want to help them by extending credit, we cannot always do this.

Unfortunately, your credit rating does not allow us to offer credit terms at this time, but we look hopefully to the future.

In the meantime, we can offer full service on a basis of cash-with-order.

We hope to hear from you soon.

Sincerely,

Dear Mr. Shulkin:

Thank you for your purchase order No. C-472 of October 3, 19__. We have no credit information on you and our normal sources show none.

This order can be expedited by your mailing us a check for the full amount of $_____, which includes prepaid shipping charges.

We look forward to filling your order.

Sincerely,

CREDIT REFUSED, PERSONAL GUARANTY

Dear Mr. Almond:

We greatly appreciate the order you gave our Mr. Robbins. You will find that we have reason to be proud of our quality products.

We want to work with you and help you get established, but from the information we have been able to gather, your firm appears to be under-capitalized, which would make it difficult for you to meet our payment terms.

One temporary solution we might suggest is for you to personally guarantee payment of your purchases. Later, we can work together on other arrangements.

Please let us hear from you soon.

Sincerely,

Dear Mrs. Warush:

When a person starts a new business, one of the difficult problems is how to establish sufficient credit to get the operation moving ahead. One solution is to provide a personal guaranty: your personal assets would support your promise to pay.

If you can do this, we will gladly fill your present order.

Please call us as soon as convenient to discuss this suggestion. I am sure we can arrive at a mutual agreement.

Sincerely,

Dear Mr. Kellup:

Thank you for your first order. We appreciate your confidence in our ability to fill it properly.

Based upon the credit information we have been able to obtain, we will need a personal guaranty (a joint personal guaranty from you and your wife) before we can start the production of your order.

We have enclosed a standard form and a postpaid envelope for its return.

We look forward to an early return of the guaranty form, after which we will immediately start work on your order.

Sincerely,

CREDIT REFUSED, SLOW PAY

Dear Mr. Pappas:

It is pleasing to learn that you are still interested in Allen's high quality tools. We received your order on October 22.

You may recall that when you last purchased goods from us, we had a difficult time getting payment from you. In fact, some of your account was turned over to Dun & Bradstreet's collection department.

We realize, however, that times and conditions change, and we should probably not be concerned. To relieve the concern we do have, please send us a few current credit references and a recent financial statement.

If you are in a rush for the tools ordered, please send us a check for $928.51. We still maintain the prompt delivery service you are familiar with.

Thank you for considering us again, and we hope to hear from you right away.

Sincerely,

Dear Mr. Bankhead:

I am completely honest when I say that many of our customers prefer to pay cash. This relieves them of any anxiety about having to make late payment charges. I would like to suggest this method to you, because, as hard as I have tried, I just can't find a way to add you to our list of credit customers at this time.

The information we have gathered indicates that your payments have consistently been getting further and further behind during the past year. This may have been a bad year for you, but we cannot see adding to your outstanding debts. We hope that conditions soon improve for you.

We do, however, appreciate your considering us as a supplier. We will be most happy to do business with you on a cash-with-order basis. You will find both our service and our products outstanding.

Sincerely,

Dear Mr. Goodall:

We greatly appreciate your interest in obtaining an American Chicken franchise. Our present expansion rate exceeds our most optimistic expectations.

We of course make credit checks on all potential franchisers, and our information indicates that you might have difficulty meeting our payment terms for merchandise and supplies to be purchased from us. These payment terms must be met as well as those for the expected loan on the purchase price.

Cash flow problems can be overcome, and we anticipate that your financial condition will improve soon. Perhaps we can review another application from you in the near future.

Sincerely,

CREDIT REFUSED, BAD RISK

Dear Mr. Colson:

Thank you for your application for credit at Barrow's Wholesale Paints. We appreciate your interest.

Your personal references are exceptionally good, and your record of hard work indicates that your business prospects are good for the near future. At present, however, with your current asset to current liability ratio being 1 to 4 rather than the usually accepted 2 to 1, we cannot extend the $5000 open credit you requested.

Please come in and talk to me at your convenience. I am sure we can set up a program of gradually increasing credit that will benefit both of us. Meanwhile, remember that deliveries on a cash purchase are made within two days.

Let me hear from you soon. We are interested in your business venture.

Sincerely,

Dear Mr. Blair:

We appreciate your interest in Sampson's and your desire to establish credit with us.

However, based on reports from our numerous sources of credit information, we can make shipments to you only when cash is received with your order.

We are sorry for this, but we are sure you understand. If we can be of any further service to you, please let us know.

Sincerely,

Dear Mr. McKenna:

Your request for a credit account with us is appreciated.

The credit information we have been able to secure from credit agencies, however, is not favorable.

Because conditions may change for the better, please let us hear from you then. We always welcome new, prompt-paying customers.

Sincerely,

Dear Mr. Glazman:

Thank you for your interest in renewing your former line of credit.

At this time we are unable to do that, but many of our products are available from your local Acme Wholesale Supply outlet. Give them a call.

Sincerely,

Dear Mr. Mairet:

Thank you for your credit application. We are always pleased to consider requests for credit from those wishing to purchase from us.

Our normal investigation has turned up the fact that you have an unusually large number of current obligations when comparing them with your reported income and receivables.

With reluctance we therefore must decline your request for credit at this time.

When your financial picture improves, please get in touch with us again.

We will be glad to deliver on a cash-before-shipment basis. Let us know if we can help you that way.

Sincerely,

CREDIT CANCELED

Comments

A letter canceling credit should be a straightforward statement of that fact. By this time your customer knows payments have been long delayed, therefore this letter will be no surprise.

However, the door should be kept open for the possibility of reinstating credit. Business and business conditions change. You and your sales representative should exchange information from time to time about the progress of this customer. You both want him back.

Dear Mr. Watson:

I am sorry, but we have had to stop extending credit to Watson Warehouse. The enclosed statement, of which you have received several copies over the past year, shows a balance due us of $5126.20. Because of the size and age of this past due amount, I am sure you can appreciate our decision.

This situation can be changed, however, with a payment of $5126.20 and copies of your current financial statements, after which we will consider extending credit again.

Sincerely,

Dear Mr. Steller:

We sincerely appreciate the opportunity you have given us to be of service to you.

Our customers are important to us and we dislike losing them. However, you have been constantly late in paying our invoices over such a long period of time that we now must ship any further orders on a cash-with-order basis.

When your account is fully paid, we will be happy to again consider providing you with a line of credit.

Sincerely,

Dear Mr. Guse:

Following our recent review of your credit history, we concluded that we can no longer extend credit to you.

Future orders will be accepted on a cash-with-order basis only. We believe this will keep your financial situation from getting out of control. Cash discounts will continue to be available along with our service policy.

We anticipate that this condition will be short-lived and that we will, in the future, be able to renew your line of credit.

Sincerely,

Dear Mr. Haueter:

Because our collection department has struggled unsuccessfully this last year to get your payments up to date, we must regretfully discontinue your credit.

For the time being, our merchandise is available on a cash or C.O.D. basis. That way we can continue to serve you.

Sincerely,

CHAPTER 10

Special Credit Letters, Business to Business

Although the special credit letters in this chapter are not as commonly written as the models in Chapter 9, their importance is just as great. Writing letters that accept payment by a promissory note or one extending a customer's payment time may be a requisite to retaining an account. Requests for special information, such as financial data, account balances, and collateral must be made. Payments made with problem checks need to be investigated, and misunderstandings require reconciliation.

Goodwill is essential. Thank your customer for his prompt payments, explain your own errors, and send a holiday greeting. When your customer begins to believe you are reasonable and appreciative, that is the start of an enduring relationship.

HOW TO DO IT

1. State the reason for your letter in the first sentence.
2. Clarify the situation or problem.
3. Suggest a solution.
4. Ask for the reader's cooperation.

CREDIT RENEWED

Dear Mr. Lime:

It is always a pleasing experience to renew the credit of a customer.

We are confident that your business has improved enough to earn a new line of credit. Our investigation suggests a starting figure of $_____.

Please keep us informed of your continuing progress so we can keep abreast of your credit needs.

We appreciate your efforts to improve your financial condition, and you can count on us to do what we can to help you.

Sincerely,

Dear Mr. Kelly:

Your recent request to re-open your line of credit has been granted. The limit is set at $_____. We hope our renewed relationship will be mutually beneficial. The decision to re-open was made after detailed consideration by our management group. We had problems with your account in the past and will watch your payment dates closely. No exceptions to our terms of net 30 days can be allowed.

On the positive side, we anticipate no difficulty working together.

Sincerely,

Dear Ms. Sperl:

After reviewing your recent credit information, we welcome you again as a credit customer.

Your recent order will be handled immediately.

Your credit limit is $_____, and we will expect strict adherence to it and to our terms of net 30 days.

We are happy to be of service to you again.

Sincerely,

PAYMENT BY NOTE

Dear Mr. Abrams:

We appreciate your explanation of your recent delay in making payments.

To help make your payments less burdensome, we would like to suggest a promissory note. This way you will make monthly payments of $290.00, which will include interest at prime rate plus 3%.

This will ease your payment problem and maintain your credit rating.

Two copies of the note are enclosed for your signature. Please return one to us.

Sincerely,

Dear Mr. Howe:

We would like to make the payment of your overdue account easier for you. Your checks have arrived at irregular intervals and for varying amounts. We need a schedule we can count on.

We would like to put the balance due into a promissory note. You would make regular monthly payments small enough that they would put no strain on your finances. The payments would include principal and interest. We suggest a monthly payment of $220.00.

Is this agreeable with you? Please let us hear from you this week. The note is enclosed for your signature.

With regards,

PAYMENT AMOUNT QUESTIONED

Dear Mr. Sanders:

Thank you for your check No. 2341 of March 9, 19__ for $1204.00.

We are holding this check because it is marked "Payment in full." Our records, however, show a balance due of $1404.00.

We suggest that you stop payment on your check and send us another in the amount of $1404.00.

Please let us know if this is more than a clerical error. If there is a problem, we wish to discuss it with you so we may come to a mutual agreement on the correct amount.

Sincerely,

Dear Mrs. Barner:

Your check No. 47210 dated November 19, 19___ in the amount of $1205.30 arrived today.

A review of our records indicates that the total amount due on November 19 was $1003.10. Please let us know what the additional $202.20 covers.

If, however, you agree with our figures, do you want a check for the difference, or do you want it credited to your account? Please let us know your preference.

Sincerely,

TIME EXTENSION GRANTED

Comments

For certain customers, it may be better to extend the time allowed for payment than to lose the customer entirely. Each case requires a separate judgment. A time may come, however, when these extension periods become unreasonable. Then you must firmly but politely tell your customer that this is the end. If your customer's request for extended terms is beyond bounds, you will have to deny the request in the first place.

Put your restrictions or denials in the middle of the letter, between an appreciative introduction and an effort to keep negotiations open. Your customer may recover.

Dear Mr. Mylars:

Your letter of March 22, 19___ is appreciated. Your frankness in relating your recent tragedy and its effect on your business is commendable.

Even the best-run businesses can run into financial difficulties when hit by circumstances beyond the manager's control. You can count on our cooperation.

We will not require payment on your account for the next three months, after which we will talk to you again about your progress toward normal operations.

Regards,

_____

Dear Mr. Maynard:

Your letter of June 2, 19___ reminds us that no business always operates smoothly. We appreciate your current position, and will do what we can to help you.

Your present payments, however, are 120 days past due, and there is a limit to how much longer we can accept your delays.

We will not press you for another 60 days. That should give you time to restructure your financing. We will hear from you by then.

Sincerely,

_____

Dear Ms. Walters:

Your frank letter of January 4, 19___ is appreciated. We realize that business circumstances are not always favorable, but your past record allows us to retain our faith in your ability to recover.

We will cooperate by allowing you an extended time in which to make your payments.

We suggest weekly payments of $130.00 on your $2600.00 debt. That will maintain your good credit standing.

Sincerely,

_____

TIME EXTENSION ENDED

Dear Mrs. Kingston:

Your recent problems are ones we can relate to, but they have resulted in non-payment of your account. We have already extended your payments beyond what we consider reasonable.

Now we must decline any further requests for delays. We expect a payment within seven days. Only then can we look to a future relationship.

Sincerely,

Dear Mr. Carey:

In our efforts to help you, we have extended your payment schedule many times during the past year and a half, yet your payments have lagged behind even the extended dates.

We are sorry but we can make no further extensions of time and can grant no additional credit.

Based on your current extended payment plan, your account will be due in full on ___(date)___. We will look for your payment by then.

Sincerely,

Dear Mr. Dotta:

We can appreciate your concern about not being able to pay your invoices according to our terms of 1% 30 days net 31 days, which are standard in the industry. We are fully aware that financial difficulties are not a rarity.

The time has come, however, when we can no longer carry your account. Perhaps a banking institution could be of assistance.

Pending your financial help, we are requesting a partial payment of $_____ by ___(date)___.

Sincerely,

Dear Mr. Bradeen:

We have reviewed your letter of March 12, 19__ requesting a change in your payment terms to 10th Prox., payable from monthly statements. You did not mention discounts.

Monthly statements can be mailed about the 5th of the following month if requested. That, however, would not change our terms of 1% ten days net 30 days, applicable to each invoice. These terms are standard in our industry.

Let us know if you will find monthly statements helpful.

Sincerely,

Dear Mr. Meure:

We are always happy to increase credit limits when it is in the best interest of our customers. Additional credit allows room for expansion, but the overuse of credit can lead to financial problems.

In our considered judgment, your credit limit is at its maximum now. When you can provide information that indicates an improvement in your ability to handle a higher credit limit, we will welcome that opportunity to review your account again.

Let's keep on working together.

Sincerely,

Dear Mr. Frere:

Through our salesman, Mr. Toby, you have requested a larger credit limit.

Having reviewed your most recent financial statements and payment records, we have concluded that you are not quite ready for an increase in your line of credit.

We will periodically review your credit condition and keep you informed.

Thank you for your continued confidence in our products.

Sincerely,

UNIDENTIFIED PAYMENTS

Comments

Unidentified payments or deductions must be checked to locate the error, which could belong to either party. Determine what you can at your end, and if that reveals no explanation, list the facts you have in a letter of inquiry to your customer. He will be as willing as you to get the records straight.

If your customer appears to be taking or has habitually taken unearned discounts or erroneous deductions, put the details in your letter and request an additional payment. Be courteous but specific.

Dear Mr. Sanger:

We received your check No. 1236 dated February 14, 19__ for $3124.96.

We are unable to identify the invoices you are paying with this check.

Please send us a list of each invoice this check covers, detailing by invoice any discounts taken or late charges paid.

We appreciate your cooperation.

Sincerely,

Dear Mr. Haffner:

Your check No. A-14772 dated October 12, 19__ in the amount of $2500.00 has been received.

We are unable to identify which invoices you intended to pay, because no reference was made to invoice numbers, dates, or corporate divisions from which you made purchases.

If this payment covers specific invoices, please mail us a list showing invoice numbers and amounts.

Because of the even dollar amount of your check and the odd-cents amounts of most of our invoices, this appears to be a payment on account. If this is the case, we will apply the payment to the oldest invoices outstanding.

Please let us know today which you intended.

Sincerely,

Dear Mr. Wellner:

Your check No. F-4111 dated July 10, 19__ was within our discount period for the invoices listed on the check stub. We thank you for your promptness.

The check total, $42,291.10 does not equal the sum of invoice amounts less the discounts allowable.

We have computed the discounts invoice by invoice and listed them on the attached sheet. If you disagree with our calculations, please send us an explanation of your computations. If, however, you agree with us, please mail a check today for the $42.14 still due.

Thank you for your cooperation.

Sincerely,

CREDIT VISIT REQUESTED

Comments

In a letter requesting information, whether it be for a credit visit, for financial statements, for collateral, for account balances, or for other data you need, make it as short as possible. However, don't be curt; include enough pleasantness to elicit the information you are requesting.

Explain why you want the information, and, if it may be helpful to your reader, the use to which it will be put. End the letter with an expression of appreciation or cooperation.

Dear Ms. Valley:

It has been our experience that a more meaningful and cordial credit relationship results from personal visits than from printed policies. Having visited personally, phone conversations between two people seem more "real."

With this in mind, I will call next week to see if we can arrange a time for me to visit you. If you have any problems we can work on or suggestions to make, we could go over them then.

I am looking forward to meeting you.

Cordially,

Dear Mr. Noblitt:

Members of our credit department like to make occasional visits to our customers' places of business. This gives us an insight into how we can be of better service to you, and, frankly, often works wonders in cementing relationships and expanding goodwill from the viewpoint of both parties.

Could you arrange such a meeting for me and my assistant? The time would be at your convenience, of course.

Cordially,

FINANCIAL STATEMENTS FROM ACCOUNTANT

Dear Mr. Osmond:

As your business grows, your credit needs tend to increase. We have found with many of our customers that an annual review of their financial data often results in our raising their credit limit.

A convenient way to provide this financial information is for your accounting firm to send us a copy of your financial statements as they are completed each year. We will then let you know of any changes in your credit limits.

All that is required of you is to sign the enclosed authorization forms, then send one to your accountant and one to us.

Your financial statements will be held strictly confidential, and you may discontinue this procedure at any time.

Two postpaid envelopes are enclosed for your convenience.

Sincerely,

Dear Mr. Axtel:

It would help us with our annual review of your credit limit if you would request your accounting firm to send a copy of your financial statements directly to us.

This would also expedite your receipt of our review.

Your help in establishing this procedure would be greatly appreciated.

Sincerely,

COLLATERAL REQUESTED

Dear Mrs. Washburn:

Thank you for your recent order and your interest in adding our company to your list of suppliers.

Although immediate credit can be given only to companies with an established high credit rating, we can work out a plan for granting you credit if you have sufficient collateral or security.

Please call so that we can schedule a meeting to discuss this possibility. Other firms have found this arrangement helpful.

Sincerely,

Dear Mr. Kading:

In recent months we have noticed that your account balance has gotten well above our established credit limits. This often happens during a period of expansion or slow payments by your customers. We are concerned about your paying, and think it is time to start a program to reduce your over-extended credit balance.

We propose an installment schedule for reducing the overdue amount. We can then continue your present line of credit providing our payment terms are met and we can obtain collateral.

We will call you next week to discuss this idea and work out the details.

Sincerely,

Dear Mr. Sunde:

With great interest we have been watching your company's rapid growth. We believe we can be of assistance by increasing your credit line.

To do this during a period of fast expansion, we would need some form of security or collateral.

Let us get together to talk over such an arrangement. Give me a call. We would both benefit.

Meanwhile, keep up your good work.

Sincerely,

ACCOUNT BALANCE REQUESTED

Dear Mrs. Calhoun:

Our auditing firm annually tests our receivables by verifying a random selection of account balances as of September 30 each year.

Will you please fill in the information requested below? Your cooperation is greatly appreciated. A business reply envelope is enclosed.

Unpaid payables balance at September 30, 19___

for ___(your company)___ .

$_____

Signature _____

Title or position _____

Sincerely,

Dear Mr. Hoyt:

Our auditing firm is making its annual examination of our financial statements.

At the close of business on October 31, 19___, our records show your company owing us $_____.

Please indicate your answers to these two questions:

_____ The amount stated above is correct.

_____ We show the amount owed to be $_____.

_____
Signed

A postage paid envelope is enclosed for your convenience in returning this letter.

Sincerely,

_____

Dear Mr. Brunet:

Regarding ___(company name)___ .

The above firm is one of our credit customers. Because their accounts receivable is part of the collateral backing a line of credit from us, we periodically verify their receivables balance.

Their records show that on August 31, 19__ you owed them $_____. If your records agree, no further action is required.

If your records do <u>not</u> confirm this balance, please fill in the balance below, and return this letter in the enclosed envelope.

Thank you for your cooperation. It is appreciated.

Sincerely,

Our records show $_____ owing to

___(company name)___ as of August 31, 19__ .

Signature_____

Title_____

DATA AVAILABLE ELSEWHERE

Dear Mr. Barrester:

Refering to your letter of May 25, 19___, if you phone Mr. Sanders at our Sacramento, California plant (000-000-0000) he will be able to give you general information about our credit experience with Almo Corporation. He has credit responsibility for that account.

It is our policy not to provide written information about our customers. I am sure, however, that Mr. Sanders can help you.

Sincerely,

Dear Mr. Blair:

We received your letter of March 15, 19___ requesting our credit experience with Danning Bros., Inc. Your letter has been forwarded to our headquarters in Chicago.

Although our company restricts the credit data it releases, our Chicago office will provide information that will help you.

Sincerely,

CREDIT BALANCE IN ACCOUNT

Dear Mr. Stout:

Due to items you returned to us on October 7 and 9, 19___ we have a credit balance in your account of $_____. Perhaps it is time for another order from you. We are here to help you with your supply needs.

Sincerely,

Dear Mr. Simpson:

For six months we have carried a credit balance in your account in the amount of $297.20. This was an adjustment to freight charges that your purchasing agent negotiated with our salesman.

We would prefer to have this offset with an order, but since it has been on our books for six months, we will mail you a check if you wish. Let us know.

Sincerely,

_____

GUARANTOR'S NOTICE

Dear ___(guarantor)___ :

On December 9, 19__ you signed a statement guaranteeing the payments of Carman's Corners.

As of this date Carman's Corners' past due account amounts to $_____. According to the guaranty, we have the right to request that you pay that amount.

We will press no further for another ten days, until August 21, 19__. In the interim, we suggest you contact Carman's Corners and request that they pay this account.

Sincerely,

_____

Dear ___(guarantor)___ :

We appreciate your cosigning for the payments of ___(company)___ on ___(date)___ .

With regret we inform you that we may have to take advantage of that guaranty.

The past due payments of ___(company)___ now amount to $_____. We can wait only 20 days before taking further action.

Sincerely,

_____

UNSIGNED CHECK

Comments

Unsigned and postdated checks present problems that require special handling. Unsigned checks can be returned to the maker, and if you detect a pattern of receiving such checks, admonish the customer. You might receive your money sooner, however, if you succeed with another procedure. Many debtors and banks will authorize payment through a "signature on file" procedure. You write to your customer stating that you intend to deposit the unsigned check (identify it clearly) as signature on file and respectfully request that your customer notify his bank to pay the check when presented.

Postdated checks are a promise to pay—not now but in the future. You can explain that these delayed payments are unfair to your other customers and reaffirm your late payment policies. On the other hand, a promise of future payments is better than intermittent, constantly delayed payments or none at all.

Dear Mr. Dankin:

Your check of March 2, 19__ is enclosed. It is being returned because it is not signed. Please sign and return it today.

This is the third check in four months that you have sent to us unsigned. This seems to be a trend that we cannot continue to accept. If we are to keep on doing business together, we must have prompt payment of our invoices.

Sincerely,

Dear Mr. Pike:

We are returning your check No. 8824 dated November 3, 19__ for your signature, which somehow was omitted.

Please sign and mail it today because you took the one-percent discount, and the discount period ended the day before the check was dated.

We assume these delays were oversights, and we will not request an additional payment, provided your signed check is returned to us <u>today</u>.

Sincerely,

_____

POSTDATED CHECKS

Dear Mr. Avery:

We wish to thank you for the business you have given us over the past three years. Your practice, however, of paying with postdated checks extends our terms of 1% 30 days net 31 days.

In fairness to our customers who pay within our terms, we can no longer continue to favor you with an extended time for payment.

I am sure you understand our position and will now pay with currently dated checks.

Sincerely,

_____

Dear Mr. Booker:

Thank you for your order No. 1334 of May 3, 19___. You enclosed your check No. 4474 postdated to May 29.

As we have attempted to make clear before, we cannot make immediate shipments on a cash-with-order basis when your checks are postdated.

We must have a current check, or, if you prefer, we can hold shipment until the date of your check. Please let us know your preference.

Sincerely,

_____

Dear Mr. Crosson:

Yesterday we received four postdated checks totaling $400.00, which we will apply to your balance

By accepting these, we are in effect extending your payment period beyond our usual terms. We will allow this one exception under two conditions.

First, if any check does not clear the bank, your remaining balance will become immediately due and collectible.

Second, all future purchases will be paid for before delivery.

We appreciate your efforts to clear your account.

Sincerely,

NSF (NON SUFFICIENT FUNDS) CHECKS

Comments

Checks returned by your bank can be handled in different ways. You may redeposit the check hoping it will clear the second time through, or you may hold the check and request your customer to issue a new one or mail a cashier's check or money order. You could send the check to your customer's bank with a cover letter requesting the bank to hold the check until funds are available to cover it. The bank will, of course, charge a fee for that service.

Dear Mr. Burns:

Your check of August 10, 19__ was returned by your bank for insufficient funds.

We will redeposit your check on August 19. Please make sure that your bank account will cover the amount of the check, which is $120.22.

Sincerely,

Dear Mr. Ames:

Your check No. 1472 dated March 15, 19__ in the amount of $778.99 has been returned twice by your bank for insufficient funds.

Please mail us a certified or cashier's check for $778.99 today.

Sincerely,

Dear Ms. Hedges:

We are enclosing your check No. 1147 for $97.20 because it was returned by your bank marked NSF. A call to your bank revealed that your account is closed. Perhaps you closed the account not realizing this check was still outstanding.

Please mail us another check today for $97.20.

Sincerely,

Dear ___(local banker)___ :

The enclosed check No. 1478 dated July 21, 19__ in the amount of $721.44 written by Mo's Motors was returned to us by your bank for insufficient funds.

Please accept this for collection. When the amount has cleared, please mail us your check for the above amount less the collection fee.

We appreciate your handling this for us.

Sincerely,

Dear Mr. Swenning:

Due to your continuing habit of paying with NSF checks, we can no longer accept your personal or business checks.

From now on, all orders must be accompanied by cash or a cashier's check.

Although many of your checks have been accepted by the bank on the second or third deposit, this creates extra work, bank charges, and a lowering of your credit rating.

We are sure you understand our requirement for cash or bank check.

Sincerely,

Comments

Many states have civil and criminal codes that apply to persons intending to defraud by drawing or delivering a check for the payment of money when a balance is nonexistent or insufficient to cover the check.

Penalties vary greatly among the states. Arizona's penalty is twice the amount of the check, maximum $50; Hawaii's is triple damages; Virginia's is triple damages, maximum $100; Indiana, Missouri, Montana, Nevada, Oregon charge triple damages not to exceed $500. Mississippi has a sliding scale.

These penalties are subject to change when state codes are revised and when particular conditions come into play.

Note: Before attempting to enforce any penalties, consult an attorney to avoid being subjected to allegations of extortion in an attempt to collect the debt.

The following letter cites California Civil Code. It must be sent by Certified Mail—Return Receipt Requested:

Dear Mr. Walther:

Subject: Dishonored Check(s)
    Check Number:
    Check Date:
    Check Amount:
Sir:

The above check has been returned by your bank. Pursuant to California Civil Code, section 1719, demand is hereby made upon you to pay the same amount in cash to this office immediately as agent representing the interests of the above creditor. Payment must be made within thirty (30) days following this certified written demand. If you fail to make such payment, then in addition to the amount owing, you may be liable for treble damages but not more than $500.00 plus principal.

Please be guided accordingly and send the money now in order to avoid these additional damages.

Very truly yours,

Comments

The state of Arizona has statutes containing both civil and criminal penalties for persons writing checks with insufficient funds or drawn on nonexistent or closed accounts.

It may be wise to consult an attorney or, if the claim is small, file it with a Small Claims Court.

> **Before turning to the criminal system, civil remedies might be attempted. If informal collection procedures fail, you can prepare a formal demand for payment. It must be personally delivered or sent Certified Mail—Return Receipt Requested. A Phoenix, Arizona attorney, Van O'Steen, suggests the following form for the formal demand letter.**

Gentlemen:

Notice of Insufficient Funds Check:

This is an official notice to you that the following described check was returned to the Payee because of insufficient funds on deposit to pay the check.

    Payor:
    Payee:
    Amount of Check:
    Date of Check:
    Check Number:
    Financial Institution on
        Which Check Was Drawn:

This notice is given to you pursuant to Arizona Revised Statutes, Section 12-671. If you fail, within twelve days of receiving this notice, to pay the check, it shall be prima facie evidence of your intent to defraud the Payee.

        Date_____

        _____
          (signature)

MISUNDERSTANDING

Dear Mr. Donaldson:

We are sorry to learn of your unsatisfactory experience with our Mr. Hanson's letters, but the bearings that we manufactured and delivered to you in Waterford became your property.

When Mr. Hanson and I visited you on February 17, 19__, there was no question that these bearings were left on consignment at your Waterford warehouse until 19__ and were used at that time by your customer, Central Trailer. The only unanswered question on your part was the problem of your pending bankruptcy and when you would be able to settle all the outstanding items. This was stated in your letter of February 14, 19__.

As far as we are concerned, Mr. Donaldson, these bearings were purchased by you and used by your customer. Our position has not changed, and this invoice, No. 43332, in the amount of $3459.90, is still outstanding. Please mail your check today.

Sincerely,

Dear Mr. Geisler:

From your letter of July 7, 19__ we believe there has been a misunderstanding about how we compute interest on your note. The note, which you signed, states that interest will be included in each monthly payment at prime rate plus four percent.

Probably the confusion arises from the fact that the prime rate changes at irregular intervals and in some months more than once. Your interest is computed on the number of days in the month that the prime rate remains at each level.

If you need a more detailed explanation, we will have our accounting department mail you the worksheet for your note, and then you can discuss the details with our accountant.

We hope this dispels the confusion. Thank you for bringing it to our attention.

Sincerely,

Dear Mr. Laico:

Last June at your request we granted you sixty-day terms on purchases over a three-month period. You were aware that that was a temporary exception to our regular terms of net 30 days.

We notice that invoices of October, November and December were paid from 50 to 70 days after the invoice date.

Did you not understand that the 60-day terms were for three months only?

We request that you pay within our regular terms of net 30 days.

Sincerely,

Comments

Thank you's, apologies, and seasonal greetings are goodwill letters. These may be letters you don't <u>have</u> to write, but you should. They make customers happy, and customers like you for that.

The considerate thoughts you have for your customers will reveal themselves in your letter. Remember, people buy from people they like.

THANKS FOR MAINTAINING ACCOUNT

Dear Mr. Solomon:

Thank you.

You're the kind of customer Richart's is proud to have. We appreciate the prompt manner in which you've paid all our invoices.

Sincerely,

Dear Mr. Dillman:

A special thanks to you, Mr. Dillman. During the past two years you have paid every one of your invoices within the discount period.

We wish to express our sincerest appreciation for your consistent timeliness.

Sincerely,

THANKS FOR PARTIAL PAYMENT

Dear Mr. Emerson:

Thank you for your recent payment of $500.00 on your account. We appreciate your efforts to clear your old balance.

You still have, however, an outstanding balance of $341.00, and we know you want to clear that amount as soon as possible.

We look forward to another payment by the end of this week.

Sincerely,

Dear Mrs. Burch:

The partial payment on your account that we received this morning is most welcome. We hope this means you will once again be making regular payments until your account is current.

The worst of your financial difficulties should be over now, and we will look for another payment by the 10th of next month.

Sincerely,

DELAYED REFUND

Dear Mr. Sanders:

I am sorry you had to wait so long for your credit of $73.95. We had some difficulties tracing the sale and the return of part of the merchandise. The refund check to you is now in the mail. Again, please excuse our delay.

Sincerely,

Dear Mr. Timmerman:

Your refund check in the amount of $120.00 is enclosed. We are sorry for any inconvenience the delay has caused you.

Sincerely,

APOLOGY

Dear Mr. Rumsey:

May we apologize for the past due notice we recently mailed to you? We realize it is exasperating to get a dun when it is not deserved.

We will strive hard to prevent such an occurrence in the future.

Cordially,

Dear Mrs. Lundgren:

We appreciate your calling our attention to your dissatisfaction with our credit policy.

Although our policies are definite and written in policy manuals, judgment in interpreting them is sometimes lacking.

We have corrected the decision about which you rightfully complained. We wish you to harbor no ill feelings and to accept our sincere apology.

Cordially,

HOLIDAY GOODWILL

Dear Mr. Michaels:

During the year in the rush of events, we tend to overlook our many friendships that are the foundation of business relationships. One of the pleasures of the Holiday Season is the opportunity to exchange greetings with those whose goodwill we value so highly.

In this spirit, we wish to express our appreciation for the pleasant association we enjoy with you.

Cordially,

Dear Mr. Jenkins:

The late fall holiday season is the jolliest time of the year. It is then that we look back and reminisce about all the good things that have happened.

We would like to pop in for a short visit, but, that being impractical, please accept this thank you note as a humble substitute.

We thank you for the business you have given us this year, and we hope to continue being of service to you.

For a moment perhaps we could put business aside and let our thoughts of this season fill us with joy.

Cordially,

CHAPTER *11*

Reminder Collection Letters, Business to Business

REMINDERS

A first reminder should be just that: a gentle suggestion that payment may have been overlooked.

An effective yet simple way to send a friendly notice is to mail a copy of your statement or invoice with a printed sticker attached.

You can obtain even more effective results by writing comments with colored felt pens on your invoices or statements.

The reminder that got the fastest results of all those we have encountered was the word "PAY" printed by hand in red felt pen covering the entire statement.

One word of caution: Don't let these messages get "cute" or you may find yourself writing such things as, "Paying old invoices will make you feel young again. Won't you take your medicine today?"

The following is a sampling of attention-getting phrases, some of which are available from stationery stores on printed stickers:

Past due—we would appreciate your payment TODAY.

Second request.

Please send payment.

Please send your check today.

Please remit.

Please remit immediately.

Please don't jeopardize your good credit.

Two months overdue.

We're expecting a check today.

Prompt pay will be appreciated.

Overlooked?

Just a reminder—your account is past due.

Prompt payment builds credit.

We helped you—please help us.

Invoices due in thirty days.

Now due and payable.

Past due.

Past due—please pay.

Thank you.

50% payment will be appreciated if you cannot pay in full today.

Last payment was received in September—could you please make a 25% payment?

Unless your previous balance shown here has been paid, it is overdue. Won't you please pay it today?

This account is overdue.

Payment due—May payment is missing.

Overdue—please pay this week.

Courtesy notice. Payment on your account is now past due. We trust this is an oversight and will appreciate your immediate attention to this account. No payment received for sixty days.

Could you make a 50% payment on this?

PAY.

FIRST COLLECTION LETTERS

If you find that one or two reminders don't do the job, your next step is to write a first-stage collection letter. This is still basically a reminder. Your reader should know after reading the first sentence, however, that it is a collection letter. Make your presentation straightforward, short and simple. A longer letter that includes explanations and appeals can be put off until the third letter.

HOW TO DO IT

1. State or imply that this is a collection letter.
2. Mention data relevant to the situation: what you are asking for, how your reader can be helped, and reasons for paying now.
3. Make the request for payment.

JUST A REMINDER

Dear Mr. Wenty:

Just a reminder that your account is $132.99 past due.

We'd appreciate an immediate payment.

Sincerely,

Dear Mr. Wally:

Just a friendly reminder.

Your check for $249.50 to cover past due invoices 1344 and 1423 has not been received. You are usually prompt.

Please send your payment today.

Sincerely,

Dear Mr. Alward:

Please accept this reminder that your January invoices have not been paid. The amount due is $429.30.

Your check written today will be appreciated.

Sincerely,

Dear Ms. Sanford:

Some people like a reminder that they may have forgotten to pay a bill. Our last invoice, No. 4442, in the amount of $1120.47 was due 20 days ago. Please mail your payment today.

Sincerely,

Dear Mrs. Tolsdale:

We would appreciate receiving a check for $498.70. This will clear the balance on your statement, which you may have overlooked.

Thank you for your consideration.

Sincerely,

Accounts Payable:

Just a reminder that your invoice hasn't been paid. Perhaps the original was overlooked, or perhaps your payment of $_____ is in the mail. If not, please send your payment today or let us know now when we may expect it.

Sincerely,

Dear Mr. Simpson:

We hope you won't object to a friendly reminder that your account of $_____ is past due. Perhaps it has escaped your notice.

Please make your payment today.

Sincerely,

Dear Mr. Gehrke:

Just a reminder that our invoice No. 22443 dated March 3, 19__ has not been paid. It is now 15 days past due. Your check for $2298.58 sent in today's mail will be appreciated.

Sincerely,

Dear Mr. Frazier:

You might appreciate a reminder that our last invoice has not been paid. It is ten days past due. Please mail us a check for $199.00 today.

Sincerely,

Dear Mr. Freeman:

Just a reminder that our terms are net 30 days. It has now been 45 days since we sent our statement showing a balance of $1229.90. A check mailed today would be appreciated.

Sincerely,

Dear Mr. Hall:

This is a friendly reminder that payment on your account has not been received.

It is likely you have been busy and merely overlooked the $392.00. We feel you would like to have this bill in your "paid" file. The enclosed envelope is for your convenience. Please mail your check today.

Cordially,

Dear Mr. Arnold:

This is a routine reminder that we send as soon as an account is past due. Often a memory jogger is appreciated. The amount is $122.40.

A postage paid envelope is enclosed for your use. Please mail your check today.

Sincerely,

Dear Mrs. Armstrong:

Many of our clients appreciate a reminder that their payments are a little overdue. Your check covering February and March services has not been received. The amount due is $200.00. Please mail your check today.

Sincerely,

Dear Mr. Irving:

This is just a friendly letter to call attention to your past due balance of $475.20. It covers our invoices 1245 of May 2 and 1398 of May 27. Please mail your check today?

Sincerely,

Dear Mr. Stone:

Friendly reminder—Your insurance policy is in its grace period. The balance due is $397.50.

Please pay now.

Sincerely,

Dear Mr. Whitney:

We wish to remind you of the coming due date, July 12, 19__, of your promissory note.

The total amount due is $229.50, which includes interest of $32.40.

We will appreciate receiving your check dated on or before July 12.

Sincerely,

Dear Mr. Cody,

Many customers like a reminder when they run slightly past due.

If you have overlooked the attached invoice, please let me have your check for the $_____ balance.

If there's a problem I'm not aware of, please call me.

Sincerely,

Dear Mrs. Callis:

Two things of interest: First, we have enclosed a notice of a special purchase that can mean extra mark-up dollars for you. Take a good look at it.

Second, this offer is good only if your account is current, and we see that you are a little behind in your payments. A check today for $_____ will bring your account up to date and allow you to participate in this special.

Regards,

PAYMENT OVERLOOKED?

Comments

The "overlooked" or "oversight" collection letter is a face-saving fiction, known to both the credit manager and the debtor. Insufficient funds to meet all obligations on the due date is a more probable reason for a delay in making payment.

When written considerately, however, this letter can improve goodwill as well as move your customer toward his checkbook.

Dear Mrs. Coddington:

You may have overlooked our May 12 invoice. The attached statement shows the amount of that invoice still unpaid. Although the amount is small, we can avoid further correspondence if you pay this $39.41 today.

A postpaid envelope is enclosed for your convenience.

Sincerely,

Dear Mr. Fredrick:

May we call your attention to your past due balance that you may have overlooked? Please mail your check for $229.00 today.

Sincerely,

Dear Mr. Carrick:

The attached statement shows a balance due of $149.90. You may have overlooked this. A check mailed today in the enclosed, postpaid envelope will be appreciated.

Sincerely,

Dear Mr. Ballan:

Just a short note to call attention to your overdue invoices that you may have set aside.

We find that many customers appreciate a reminder of this sort.

Please take a moment now to write a check for $874.30.

Sincerely,

Dear Mr. Conrad:

We all forget now and then to pay a bill and appreciate a reminder.

The enclosed copy of your latest statement indicates a past due balance of $927.77.

May we expect a check from you written today?

Sincerely,

Dear Mr. Wallace:

Just a routine reminder that your account now includes a $114.31 past due balance.

We suspect this payment has been overlooked. If so, would you please process the enclosed invoice for immediate payment?

Of course, if there is some problem, we want to hear from you. If not, please mail your check today.

Sincerely,

Dear Ms. Drew:

We wish to thank you for the business you have given our company. Our customers are valued assets.

As you know, our open accounts are due on the 15th of the month following the date of purchase and are considered past due on the 16th of the same month.

We note that your balance of $481.33 is past due. We feel sure this must be an oversight on your part and that we can depend upon your mailing us a check today.

Sincerely,

Dear Mr. Merkle:

We have not received your first payment due upon signing the Bidwell contract, which was signed July 30, 19__.

Please clear this oversight by mailing your check today for $_____.

Sincerely,

Dear Mr. Jensen:

Your last invoice for $402.00 has not been paid. It is twenty days past due now and we are concerned.

Please mail a check in the enclosed envelope today.

Sincerely,

Dear Mr. Gaylord:

You have not made a payment on your March invoices, and they are now past due. If you overlooked this or need more time, let us know right away, and we will work with you to make the necessary extensions.

Otherwise, please send us your check for $2199.00 today.

Sincerely,

Accounts Payable:

Your account shows the following unpaid invoices:

Date	Number	Amount

We are enclosing copies of our invoices and would appreciate your immediate payment.

Sincerely,

Dear Mr. Wentling:

We haven't heard from you about the items on the attached statement. Payment is now fifteen days overdue. You found our service satisfactory, therefore won't you please mail your check for $722.47 today?

Sincerely,

Dear Mr. Gomez:

Our terms of 1% 10 days net 30 days have not been met. The invoices listed on the attached statement are now past due. If there is a reason for this unusual delay, please call me today. We will be glad to work with you. The amount due is $874.88. Please send at least a partial payment of $400.00 today.

Sincerely,

Dear Mr. Holmes:

"Our check is enclosed." We have been expecting these words from you for the past ten days. Please let us hear them by mailing your check for $799.50 today.

Sincerely,

Dear Ms. Lester:

Your account continues in good standing with us, except for the enclosed past due invoice for $_____.

May I have your check today?

Sincerely,

Dear Mr. Sutherland:

Your account is past due in the amount of $_____. It is imperative that you either pay the above amount or contact me immediately upon receipt of this letter.

You may call me personally at 000-000-0000.

Sincerely,

THIS IS WHAT YOU OWE

Comments

When more than one, or even only one, invoice is to be mentioned in a letter, you can make the reading easier by listing the invoices rather than including them in your descriptive message.

This little convenience is appreciated by the person checking your letter against his or her company's records.

Ladies:

A review of your account reveals the following past due invoices:

ITEM NUMBER	DATE	AMOUNT	DUE DATE
30.2234	2-4-__	$4356.77	3-4-__

If your remittance is not already en route, your assistance in expediting payment today would be appreciated.

Sincerely,

Dear Mr. Danis:

As you requested, we have enclosed a copy of the items listed below that remain open on your account:

Item Number	Date	Amount
33.6632	11/29/__	$1411.10
41.0022	12/20/__	191.80
		$1602.90

We believe this will enable you to place the above in line for payment. If additional information is needed, please let us hear from you. If not, please mail your check today.

Sincerely,

Dear Mrs. Anderson:

Could you please review the enclosed phone bill listing? Some of the calls are probably yours. We would appreciate receiving payment for the calls made by you. Your explanation and payment today would be appreciated.

Sincerely,

Dear Mr. Miller:

Your business is important to us and we welcome it, even though your orders have been small. Your June balance of $82.00 has not been paid. A payment today would make your business even more appreciated.

Sincerely,

Attn: Accounts Payable Bookkeeper:

      Re: No. 14-4588   10/12/___ $993.51

Enclosed is a duplicate copy of the above invoice.

We issued credit memo No. 1854 to cancel this invoice. You apparently used the credit to cancel the invoice and also to reduce the amount you paid on one of our later invoices.

It would be appreciated if you could review your records and if in agreement process the invoice for payment today.

Please call if we can provide additional assistance.

Very truly yours,

Dear Mr. Edwards:

      Re: Invoice No. 99-4588   1/22/___ $3355.78

According to our investigation, this invoice represents a shipment of canvas made against your order No. U-51786 dated 1/4/___.

As we discussed on May 6, we would appreciate your approving it for payment today.

Sincerely,

Dear Mr. Watson:

Your attention is directed to the attached list of freight bills, which our records indicate are unpaid beyond the credit period permitted by our tariff.

You may have already made the payment and it has simply not reached our accounting department. If these bills have not been paid, however, a prompt remittance would be appreciated. Please mail your check to West Transportation Co., P. O. Box 0000, Arlington, VA 00000.

Sincerely,

Dear Mr. Swanson:

Thank you for your partial payment of our invoice No. 77321.

For some reason you did not include the freight charge. Our terms as stated on the invoice are F.O.B. our plant.

Please review your payment records, and if you agree please mail your check today for $147.80 to cover the freight costs.

Sincerely,

SMALL BILLS

Dear Mr. Hoffert:

It is not the amount you owe, only $27.50, but your promptness in paying that determines your credit rating. Our invoice No. 2781 is now due.

To start a good credit record you must mail us your check today.

Sincerely,

Dear Mrs. Brown:

Small accounts are a convenience for a small business, and we want to help you all we can. Of course we also like to be paid so we can continue to supply you.

We hope you will mail your check for $12.00 today.

Cordially,

Dear Mr. Jorgenson:

We send you this reminder that you owe us $123.47 because we want you to order more stationery items from us after you have paid this bill. Please mail your check today.

Sincerely,

Dear Mr. Armstrong:

Losing one payment of $12.95 will not harm our business, but losing hundreds becomes a real burden. We may spend nearly $12 on letter writing alone to collect one overdue account, and that just isn't fair.

We know you don't want to appear unfair. Please mail your check today for $12.95.

Sincerely,

Dear Mrs. Radke:

Have you forgotten our invoice 7742 of April 16? Its small size does not diminish its importance to us.

Please mail your check for $19.87 today.

Sincerely,

COOPERATION

Dear Mr. Brooke:

We appreciate your business and strive to serve you well at all times.

In return, we are happy to receive your cooperation through the payment of your accounts in accordance with the terms of sale.

We look forward to your prompt payment of $_____ today.

Sincerely,

Dear Mr. Tammee:

Just a reminder that business flows smoother when the parties involved cooperate.

Specifically, we would appreciate your paying us $133.00 for your purchase of July 12, 19__, which is now 16 days past due. May we have your check today?

Sincerely,

GOOD FAITH

Dear Mr. Duffy:

Our records indicate that your past due balance of $839.96 has not been paid. Perhaps there is some misunderstanding that is preventing settlement. Your record with us has always been good and we feel sure there must be a good reason why you have permitted your account to run so long.

We would certainly appreciate having you call us, and we will try to arrange a mutually satisfactory agreement. Your immediate call to us would convince us of your good faith in settling this overdue account. Of course a check would be appreciated as well. Why not mail your check today?

Sincerely,

Dear Mr. Spalding:

Your account is now 20 days past the due date. The amount owed is $1095.90.

We indicated our faith in you when we granted you credit. In return we would appreciate the expression of your good faith by writing us a check today.

Sincerely,

DISCOUNT AVAILABLE

Dear Mr. Buys:

We have had the same experience: an invoice gets lost somewhere in the paper maze. That can cause lost discounts and reduced profits over a year's time.

Because that may have happened to our invoice No. B-22745 of January 7, 19__, we are enclosing a copy and are giving you permission to take the 2% discount if paid by February 25.

Please take advantage of this one-time extended discount period and mail. your check today.

Sincerely,

Dear Mr. Yurman:

Although our invoice No. 1246 of May 7, 19__ is past the discount period, our manager has approved your taking the cash discount if you pay it before June 7.

This is an unusual exception to our standard terms, and we feel certain you will take advantage of it. Please mail your check today.

Sincerely,

CHAPTER 12

Request Collection Letters, Business to Business

A second stage business to business collection letter should be slightly more demanding than the first letter. It is stronger than a reminder; it is a request for payment.

State that it is a second request on a past due account or that you received no response to your first letter.

A small sales pitch may be included, mentioning a new product or service, your quality product line, or perhaps your business stability.

The tone of the second letter should be friendly.

HOW TO DO IT

1. State or imply that this is a second request for payment.
2. Ask why the payment has not been made.
3. State or list the amount or amounts due.
4. Ask for prompt payment.

SECOND NOTICE

Dear Mr. Sornberger:

This is our second letter reminding you of your overdue balance of $650.00.

May we suggest that you approve payment of the total amount today before you lay this letter aside. In fact, why not mail your check today?

With regards,

Gentlemen:

We again call your attention to the following freight bills which, according to our records, are still unpaid well beyond our normal terms:

Date	Bill Number	Amount
7-19-__	74458337	$1472.00
10-22-__	74789912	2428.81
		$3900.81

We would greatly appreciate your informing us of the reason for further delay, but would prefer that you mail your check today.

Sincerely,

Dear Mr. Anson:

Enclosed are copies of past due invoices.

If your records show that these are unpaid, please let us know when we can expect payment, or mail your check today.

Sincerely,

Dear Mr. Buckley:

Although the past due invoices included with this letter were previously called to your attention, we have yet to receive any payment.

Since your account is now more than _____days beyond the original due date, there should be no further delay. Would you please mail your check today?

Sincerely,

Dear Mr. Olds:

Reference is made to our April 28, 19__ letter advising you that we expected payment of the $1,472.00 balance due on our invoice 41-1112 dated March 3, 19__. To date this amount has not been paid, and our operating people believe we should be reimbursed for the cost of repairing the door damaged by your delivery driver.

Please remit this balance today.

Sincerely,

Dear Mr. Bender:

We have not received our first progress payment of $1050.00 for the installation of your die cutting machine. The payment was due March 3, 19__. Can you get the payment procedure rolling by mailing your check today?

Sincerely,

PLEASE PAY NOW

Dear Mr. Blume:

Payment of this overdue amount today will be appreciated:

Invoice No.	Due Date	Amount
A-445	4-3-19__	$2225.40

Please mail your check today.

Sincerely,

Dear Mr. Watson:

The invoice listed below is past due:

Invoice No._____
Amount $_____
Due Date_____

Please mail your remittance today.

Sincerely,

IS THERE A PROBLEM?

Dear Mr. Duke:

We ask again, is there a reason why your payment is being delayed?

Invoice No. W-4468 dated May 14, 19__ was due on June 14, 19__. It is now 45 days late.

If there is a reason for this delay, please discuss it with us, and let us know how we may help.

Should your check have been mailed before you receive this letter, we thank you for your payment of $929.97. If not, please mail your check today.

Sincerely,

Dear Mr. Cartwright:

Is there a reason why this overdue balance has been delayed?

Invoice No	Amount	Due Date
4358	$4421.20	7-7-19__

If additional services are needed, please explain so that we may help you. Otherwise, please mail your check for $4421.20 today.

Sincerely,

Dear Mr. Fricker:

Your outstanding balance with us is $505.65.

We have not received a recent payment. Be sure to let us know if you have any questions about the amount owing.

Please mail a payment today.

Sincerely,

Dear Ms. Edison:

A second copy of your May 31 statement is attached.

Notice that credit memo No. C-472 dated May 3 has been deducted.

If there is still a problem, please let us know today.

If payment has merely been delayed, we would appreciate your payment of $307.00 today, please.

Sincerely,

Mr. Hedelsmann:

As of the date of this letter, the following items were considered past due according to our terms:

Date	Invoice No.	Amount Past Due

Total Past Due $_____

If there is a problem, please let me know if I can help. If not, we would appreciate your payment today.

Sincerely,

Dear Mr. Delmar:

This is to notify you that your overdue subscription account is delinquent. Please send payment of $48.00 today.

If there has been an error or misunderstanding, please write to us now. Otherwise, an immediate payment by you is urgently requested. Please mail your check today.

Sincerely,

Re: Invoice No. 1471 dated May 12, 19__ in the amount of $477.98.

Accounts Payable:

As of this date, our records indicate that the above-mentioned invoice is past due on your account.

Is there are problems or discrepancies with the bill, please contact me immediately at 000-0000. If not, please remit payment promptly to the address given on the invoice. Please do it today.

Sincerely,

Dear Mr. Dutton:

We again call your attention to your outstanding balance:

$1512.47

Our records show that we have not received a payment since January 14, 19__.

Your remittance at this time will be appreciated. Should there be questions concerning the above amount, please contact us today. If not, please mail your check today.

Sincerely,

Dear Mr. Stedman:

We have had no response to our recent reminder of your past due account.

We still believe the items called to your attention have either been overlooked or delayed in payment for some reason.

Won't you please let us know that reason or otherwise mail your check today?

Sincerely,

OVERLOOKED?

Dear Mr. Archer:

A statement was mailed to you on July 12, 19___. Perhaps you overlooked it. We are enclosing another copy.

Please mail your check for $1132.40 today.

Sincerely,

Dear Mr. Runyon:

You have not responded to our letter reminding you of your unpaid account of $551.99.

Please let us know if you have overlooked this payment. Perhaps there is a reasonable explanation for your delay.

We would like you to pay this account today.

Sincerely,

MISPLACED?

Dear Mr. Du Gard:

It's so easy to misplace or misfile a bill. Could that have happened to you? We ask because your account is 45 days overdue.

Please check our invoice No. 1441 of April 30 for $2295.00 and send your payment today unless you have some special reason for your delay. If you do, please call or write to us.

We look forward to receiving your reply or preferably your payment today.

Sincerely,

Dear Mrs. Lavengood:

Your account for $300.00 is 45 days overdue.

Was our invoice No. A-4011 dated March 31, 19___ misplaced?

We would appreciate your mailing your check today.

Sincerely,

SHOULD WE THANK YOU?

Attention: Accounts Payable

Ladies and Gentlemen:

No doubt it was your intention to send a payment at the time you received your February statement. This remittance must have been overlooked because your check has not been received.

If your check has already been mailed, "thank you." If there is a reason for your withholding payment, please tell us the circumstances so that some arrangement for payment can be made quickly.

Your cooperation is appreciated. A check mailed today would also be appreciated.

Sincerely,

Dear Mr. Arvin:

The attached statement shows a past due balance of $4607.12 going back as much as 60 days.

Perhaps your check has already been mailed. If so, please accept our thanks.

If it hasn't been mailed, please send your check today.

Thank you,

Dear Mr. Dobson:

Should this letter be a thank-you for your check? It should if it crossed your check in the mail.

However, if you haven't written the check yet, can we expect it by April 17? The amount due is $1899.05.

Sincerely,

Gentlemen:

Your payroll report for June 19___ has not been received.

Your continued protection depends on your prompt reporting and paying the insurance premium.

If you have already mailed your report and payment, THANK YOU. If you have not, please mail them today.

Sincerely,

THANKS FOR PARTIAL PAYMENT

Dear Mr. Van Wormer:

Please send us your planned schedule for payments on the balance of the $1500.00 in your open account.

We thank you for the payment you made on October 15 of $300.00. The remaining payments should be completed by September 30, 19___. May we suggest $300.00 every two weeks? Please mail an installment today.

Sincerely,

Dear Ms. Maxim:

Thank you for your check No. 1473 of September 2, 19___ for $120.00.

As we discussed with you, we expected to receive a schedule of future payments to pay off your balance, which is now $470.00.

May we suggest a schedule for future payments of $150.00 every two weeks, and also another payment now? Please confirm this and mail your check today.

Sincerely,

Dear Ms. Hollstrom:

Thank you for your check for $456.00 dated October 10.

We appreciate this partial payment of your overdue balance. In that same spirit of cooperation, we anticipate you will want to make another payment now.

May we expect your check today?

Sincerely,

SMALL DEBTS

Attn: Accounts Payable

Mrs. Gabler:

Frankly, we haven't discovered a way to collect your long-overdue balance of $14.10. This may be a small amount to you, but small amounts do add up to significant dollars.

We would sincerely appreciate your cooperation by mailing us a check today for $14.10.

Sincerely,

Dear Mr. Hanning:

You still haven't paid your old past due balance of $13.41. Even seemingly small amounts are important to us. Please mail your check for $13.41 immediately—today.

Sincerely,

FAIRNESS

Dear Mr. Peale:

We try hard to be equally fair with all our customers, and I am sure you wish to be fair with us. Your account now shows:

April 30	$144.10
May 31	194.70
June 30	401.05
	$739.85

Perhaps you have overlooked these past due amounts. It would be only fair to pay them now. The enclosed envelope is for your convenience. Please mail your check today.

Sincerely,

Dear Mr. Gonzales:

We think it only fair that you pay your bills according to our terms. By now you have probably resold most of your last purchase of towels.

Your account is 40 days past due in the amount of $482.10. A check mailed today would be appreciated.

Sincerely,

FRIENDSHIP

Dear Mr. Campbell:

We strive to be both friendly and successful. We can be friendly by our own efforts, but to be successful, we need your help. The amount by which you can help is $937.50, now past due. Please mail your check today.

Cordially,

Dear Mr. Botsford:

You have been a good customer for a number of years, and we try to be fair. Your account, however, remains past due.

Please help us continue this friendly relationship by mailing your check today for $8482.44.

Sincerely,

Dear Mr. Hyatt:

Even good friends need an occasional reminder—sometimes even a second one—that an account is a little past due.

We would appreciate receiving your check today for the balance due of $1101.00.

Regards,

Dear Mr. Cannady:

Just a friendly reminder—a second one—that our invoice No. 1729 dated March 3, 19__ in the amount of $6129.87 is now 25 days past due.

Your check mailed today would be a friendly gesture.

Sincerely,

Dear Mr. Southern:

Please consider this letter and the attached statement friendly but urgent reminders that your order of January 29, 19__ remains unpaid.

To avoid further correspondence, please mail your check today for $2281.45 in the enclosed, postpaid envelope.

Sincerely,

WHEN WILL YOU PAY?

Attn: Accounts Payable:

On July 12, 19___, we mailed you copies of the following invoices:

Date	Number	Amount

We have not yet received your check. Please let us know when payment will be sent. We would appreciate an early reply, and, even better, a payment. Please mail your check today.

Sincerely,

Dear Mrs. Temper:

Thank you for bringing to our attention your reasons for not paying our invoices 4412, 4415, 4622 and 4713. Our production and sales departments are investigating your questions.

In the meantime, the following undisputed invoices are also past due: 4311, 4387, 4399, 4500 and 4502.

When can we expect payment of these? We would appreciate your paying them today.

Sincerely,

HOLDING ORDERS

Dear Mr. Langley:

We have not received the balance due us of $500.50 or any response to our inquiries asking why you haven't paid.

Your two recent orders, No. 365 and 372, and future orders will be held until your balance owing is paid. Do what is best for both of us by mailing your check today.

Sincerely,

Dear Mr. Sanger:

The enclosed statement shows an overdue balance of $496.60. You have not replied to any of our inquiries or made a payment.

We must, therefore, hold your current order, No. C-2947, and all future orders until your account is cleared. Why not reestablish your credit and clear your account by mailing your check today?

Sincerely,

REDUCING COSTS

Dear Mr. Rhone:

This is our second notice of your overdue account of $1251.00.

Our costs increase when payments are delayed, and therefore so do our prices. We need your help in holding down our charges to you.

We have enclosed a postpaid envelope for your convenience in making your payment today.

Sincerely,

Dear Mr. Dean:

You could help us lower our costs and subsequently our prices by promptly paying the enclosed invoice. This is our second request.

Please use the enclosed, postpaid envelope to mail your check today.

Sincerely,

BILLING DELAYED

Dear Mrs. Yacomo:

As prearranged, we did not bill you for the self-hypnotic tapes until you had ample time to examine them. The examination period has expired.

Please complete the processing of the enclosed invoice for payment and mail your check today.

Sincerely,

Dear Ms. Manning:

SECOND NOTICE ENCLOSED

We extended to you the courtesy of not invoicing you for this audio-visual program until your full examination period had concluded. We, therefore, would appreciate your expediting this invoice for payment and mailing your check today.

Thank you,

SELLING TO PAST DUE CUSTOMERS

Dear Mr. Allen:

Thank you for your order No. 1140. It has been approved for credit and will be shipped as requested on your order.

We must remind you, though, that your account is past due. We believe you will reciprocate for our shipping your new order by making a substantial payment on your overdue balance.

Please mail your check today.

Sincerely,

Dear Mr. Wheadon:

We sent you a reminder letter three weeks ago about your past due balance of $4476.00. Since then you have made additional purchases of $1285.50.

Please put your account on a current basis by mailing us a check for $4476.00 today.

Sincerely,

REORDERS

Dear Mr. Owens:

Your account with us has a past due balance of $2257.00. With winter nearly over, you will soon be needing more building supplies.

To assure your getting them on short notice as you have in the past, please bring your account up to date by mailing us your check for $2257.00 today.

Sincerely,

Dear Mr. Megraw:

Last winter you asked us for an overnight air freight delivery of ski boots. We were happy to oblige.

We find now, however, that we must again ask for partial payment of that order. We can help you with your reorders only if you help us now.

Please mail your check today. We suggest at least $400.00.

Sincerely,

LATE CHARGES

Dear Mr. Drossell:

Thank you for your final installment payment on your contract.

We remind you again, however, that charges for late payments as well as for the spare parts you ordered are still due. These are listed on the attached statement.

It would be appreciated if you would kindly remit the balance due of $298.80 today to complete this contract.

Sincerely,

Dear Mr. Emeis:

Each month that your account goes unpaid, you incur late charges of 1% per month, which amounts to an annual rate of a shade over 12%.

A check mailed within the next three days for $_____ will save you from another month's late charges.

Sincerely,

NEW CUSTOMER

Dear Mrs. Lindeen:

You have not replied to our statements and our letter of August 2.

As a new customer, this concerns us. There must be a problem. Please let us know what it is.

If payment has just been put off, we politely request your payment of $297.29 today.

In either case, let us hear from you.

Cordially,

Dear Mr. Lacy:

This is our second letter reminding you of your past due account.

As a new customer, we are writing to let you know that it is our practice to follow-up on accounts that are not paid in accordance with our terms of 1% ten days net 25 days.

Please mail your payment today.

Sincerely,

COLLECTING FROM MINORS

Although state laws vary, in general minors are those under eighteen years of age. They may refuse to honor purchases made for their personal use. A minor engaging in business, however, is responsible for goods or services purchased. Proceed with caution and obtain legal counsel when dealing with minors.

BANKRUPTCY AND INSOLVENCY

When a debtor company becomes financially disabled, the creditors may meet and agree on terms for solving the debtor's payment problems. This keeps both sides out of the bankruptcy courts. Because of the possibility of unilateral legal action by one of the creditors in an out-of-court agreement and the legal complexities of bankruptcy, it is wise to consult an attorney before engaging in written communications concerning an insolvent or bankrupt debtor.

CHAPTER *13*

Appeals Collection Letters, Business to Business

After a reminder or two and a couple of letters have brought no response, you begin to wonder if there is a problem your debtor has withheld from you. Ask if there is a problem or reason for not having paid. Suggest possible reasons, such as slow business, not enough cash for a full payment, or personal financial difficulties. Then offer to help your customer.

This is also the letter in which you can appeal to the reader's personal motivations such as pride, duty, fear, friendship, loyalty, or fair play.

Third collection letters, because they discuss problems and solutions and make appeals, tend to be the longest.

HOW TO DO IT

1. Mention that previous efforts have been made to collect.
2. Appeal to personal motivations.

3. Agree to help overcome the debtor's problem.
4. Request prompt payment.

THIRD NOTICE

Dear Mr. Wayne:

This is our third letter asking for payment of the $799.10 past due on your account.

Will you please call me so we can discuss a way to settle this overdue amount. Several different arrangements are available, and I'm sure we can agree on one.

A phone call from you today would be appreciated.

Sincerely,

Dear Mr. Haemer:

THIRD NOTICE

Business-to-business cooperation is required if our companies are to survive. We honor your credit terms and look to you to honor ours.

However, it seems necessary to send this third request for payment of your overdue amount of $_____.

Please make out your check today.

Sincerely,

APPEAL TO CREDIT STANDING

Dear Mr. Andrus:

You have been sent several letters regarding your overdue account in the amount of $6991.45. We have had no reply from you.

Your credit rating may suffer because when other suppliers ask us for our credit experience with you, we have no choice but to report your slowness in paying.

We strongly suggest immediate payment in full or partial payment with a statement of when you will pay the balance.

Please contact us today.

Sincerely,

Dear Mr. Colston:

This is the third letter we have written you about our past due invoice AHO-4744 of last October 12 in the amount of $12,743.

Because you have been one of our best customers and have paid on time in the past, we believe there may be a problem with your ability to make full payment now.

To preserve your excellent credit record, please discuss this situation with us immediately. We can work out something together.

Sincerely,

Dear Mr. Farber:

On February 3 we mailed you a detailed statement of all unpaid invoices as you had requested.

We were expecting a prompt reply or a check from you. That was three weeks ago, and we still have no reply.

Your account is seriously past due, and that is adversely affecting your credit rating.

We are asking for full payment of $1478.94 today.

Sincerely,

Dear Mr. Carlson:

The enclosed statement of your account reflects a past due balance about which we have written to you on several occasions.

Your credit reputation with your suppliers depends upon prompt payment to each company.

We cannot understand why you have chosen to ignore our requests for payment and have put us in a position that will require direct collection action.

Please remit the past due amount of $2871.95 today in the enclosed envelope.

Yours very truly,

Dear Ms. Merz:

Your payment of $374.00 due May 10 for the step chairs purchased on April 2 is now 40 days overdue.

We notice that in the past you have paid following the second or third letter we have sent requesting payment. All future invoices must be paid within our terms of net 10 Prox. Your credit rating and our continued business relationship is at stake.

We look for your check for $374.00 within seven days.

Sincerely,

Dear Mr. Dunlap:

The attached statement includes $99.20 due tomorrow, February 12, 19__, and $145.70 due 40 days ago.

To keep your account current and your credit rating intact, please mail your check today for the total amount due, $244.90.

Sincerely,

Dear Mr. Hodges:

We were expecting your check for $2107.99 before today. On April 10, 19__ you sent us a letter (a copy is attached) stating that you would resume paying our invoices within our terms of 1% 10 days net 30.

Your account is now 100 days overdue. To protect your credit standing, you must mail your check today. I will expect it in three days.

Sincerely,

Dear Mr. Atwood:

Account Number_____
Amount in default $_____

Your past due account has been turned over to me for immediate liquidation.

All outstanding balances, whether large or small, reflect badly on your credit rating, which is circulated among your suppliers.

Please send a check today for the outstanding balance of $1471.30 and reinstate your good credit rating.

AVOID UNNECESSARY EMBARRASSMENT—MAIL YOUR CHECK TODAY.

Very Truly Yours,

APPEAL TO FAIRNESS

Dear Ms. Ryder:

We try hard to be equally fair to all our customers, and I am sure you wish to be fair with us. Your account shows:

September 30	$1452.78
October 31	2475.91
November 30	1997.90
	$5926.59

Perhaps you have been putting off paying these past due amounts. It would be only fair to pay them now. The enclosed, postpaid envelope is for your convenience. Please mail your check today.

Sincerely,

Attention: Accounts Payable

RE: PAST DUE BALANCE OF $3,000.00

Mr. Milano:

We are sorry that we must again call your attention to your unpaid balance which has been past due since last October.

Invoice No.	Date	Amount
N-12444	9-9-___	$3,000.00

Your account was opened with the understanding that we would serve you to the best of our ability and that you in turn would make payments in accordance with our regular warehouse terms, which are net thirty days. We believe that we have lived up to our part of the agreement. In fairness, we believe that you should live up to yours.

Please mail us your check for the above balance today. If your check has already been mailed, please accept our thanks.

Sincerely,

Dear Mr. Kirkpatrick:

The $96.00 you owe on your account is still overdue. We are sure you will agree it is reasonable for us to expect that those who owe us money will pay it.

Please review the enclosed bill. We believe we are being only fair by making this direct appeal for payment.

We have sent you six bills over the past six months. We trust it will not be necessary to send you any more bills. If the amount is correct, please mail your check TODAY.

Sincerely,

Dear Mr. Arliss:

We made an exception for you from our regular terms of 1% 10 days net 30 by allowing you 60 days to pay for your order of October 10, 19___.

You have now exceeded that extension by 10 days. We can allow you no more time. All future orders must be paid for within our regular terms to be fair to our other customers.

Please mail your check for $1297.20 today.

Sincerely,

APPEAL TO COOPERATION

Dear Mr. Murdock:

PLEASE GIVE YOUR IMMEDIATE ATTENTION TO THIS <u>THIRD</u> RE-MINDER of your past due invoice in the amount of $1121.05.

We have served you in good faith and hope to continue doing so, but now we must have your payment in full.

Please mail your check today.

Sincerely,

Dear Mr. Dakin:

Though your account is considerably past due, we have continued to fill your orders.

So that we may continue what has been a mutually beneficial relationship, we'll need your check in full payment of the outstanding balance.

Would you please mail that check today?

Sincerely,

Dear Mr. Jepson:

It is our policy to help our customers as much as possible. If there is a reason why your recent payments have been getting more and more behind, please let us know. We can do one or more of several things to ease your cash flow problems and at the same time maintain your credit rating.

Please let us hear from you today.

Sincerely,

Comments

Customer copies of the following letter are printed by a computer on computer paper. This technique combines an attention-getting format with light-hearted humor. The result has been improved collections.

Attention: Accounts Payable
Dear Sir/Madam or Fellow Computer:

I am Salvo Tool's computer, and I never make mistakes. However, all the information I have is given to me by one or more human beings who often do make mistakes.

My memory banks indicate that your account is overdue. This may or may not be true (I don't trust humans).

Please check your records or memory banks, and, if you agree, please remit as soon as possible.

If your records do not agree, would you please contact one of my humans at 000-000-0000 with the proper data and ask them to correct my memory banks.

It is my job to keep these humans straight (no easy task) and I must make everything come out correctly at the end of the month. If I do not hear from you by then, I have to tell my humans, and this is always a pain in my floppy disk. So please give this matter your prompt attention.

The amount in question is as follows:

             Date   Invoice   Amount

Please mail your check today.

                                        I. M. Computer
                                        Accounting Department

P. S. If the aforementioned has very recently been taken care of, please disregard this message (the Post Office has humans too).

Dear ___(client's name)___ :

I need your help in solving a problem that has been troubling me for several weeks. A self-addressed, stamped envelope is attached for your ease in replying. The problem that has been baffling me is this: Should we have dinner at 21 Turtle Club before or after our firm files suit against your corporation for unpaid fees owing us?

One of the complications, of course, is that the lawyer filing suit would wish to have a retainer. If we pay that, then it would cut down on the amount of the beverages and nourishment budget. Then again, if we do go to 21 Turtle Club first, the shock of being served with a legal notice by a constable might be intensified.

You can see from the foregoing narrative that your assistance is needed in determining the correct social amemity. So, please do respond during the next four or five days.

Sincerely,

(Reprinted with permission of <u>Public Accounting Report</u>, Atlanta, Georgia.)

APPEAL TO JUSTICE

Dear Mr. Fischer:

You are a new customer, and already your account is past due.

A continuing business relationship depends on a mutual agreement to comply with the stated terms of sale. We agree to provide quality merchandise and service. You agree to pay on time.

Your check for $749.50 should reach us within ten days.

Sincerely,

Dear Mr. Ligerman:

Our previous two letters regarding your past due balance of $910.00 have brought no response. We have heard no objections or complaints and therefore assume you have no objections to the amount due.

We feel the only just course for you is to pay what you agree you owe.

We will look for a check before the end of this week.

Sincerely,

APPEAL TO HONOR

Dear Mr. Dahlgren:

It is our policy to help customers whenever possible. We allowed you an extra 45 days to pay for your last purchase, and you promised to pay within that period.

To date we have not received your check.

We now request immediate payment. Please mail your check today for $10,420.52.

Sincerely,

Dear Mr. Merritt:

We are surprised to learn that you have not made the payment on your past due account for the month of April.

In your letter of February 4, 19___, you promised to take care of this indebtedness in monthly installments of $1225.00.

We shall expect these payments to be made on or before the 10th of each month until the entire amount is paid.

Sincerely,

Dear Mr. Chamberlain:

On August 4, 19___, you promised us a payment of $100.00 on your account by September 1, and we are still waiting for it.

Please mail your check for $100.00 in the enclosed envelope today.

Sincerely,

APPEAL TO PRIDE

Dear Mr. Casassa:

Pride of workmanship is our first consideration. We are proud of the painting and sign work we did on your building, and we know you are proud of the results.

Pride should also extend to financial obligations. Our previous reminders that payment was due have been ignored. If there are circumstances of which we are not aware, please let us know so that we can work together in solving your payment problem.

May we suggest using the enclosed, postpaid envelope to mail a half payment today.

If needed, please contact us today. It is no loss of pride to admit the need for help.

Sincerely,

Dear Mr. Koenig:

You have not replied to our reminders and two letters about your past due account of $_____.

Also, our attempts to reach you by phone have been unsuccessful.

A check from you today would add to your pride in your reputation, and it will keep your credit rating intact.

Sincerely,

APPEAL TO DUTY

Dear Mr. McKeen:

You have received several reminders and letters since your account became due.

You have sent neither the payment nor an explanation for not paying.

The time has come, Mr. McKeen, for you to take a couple minutes—today—either to tell us when we can expect your payment or to mail your check for $2297.00.

Sincerely,

Dear Mrs. Wavell:

We are surprised to learn that you have not settled your past due account in the amount of $337.92.

Further extension of time will not be possible, and we shall depend on your making full payment within ten days.

We would appreciate your taking action today.

Sincerely,

Dear Mr. Hobson:

We have exhausted every method we know of to try to get you to settle your past due balance of $3826.40.

We expect your account to be paid in full by March 14, 19__, ten days from today.

Sincerely,

APPEAL TO FEAR

Dear Mr. Barr:

You have declined to answer our many reminders, statements, and letters about your past due amount of $1772.90.

Please use the postpaid envelope enclosed for your convenience in mailing your check. That will put off our having to take any further action. Please respond today.

Sincerely,

Dear Ms. Crawford:

We have given you six months to pay your overdue balance of $422.90.

To avoid further action on our part, please mail your check for $422.90 today.

Sincerely,

Dear Mr. Chobert:

In spite of the fact that we have sent you many reminders and letters about your past due invoice No. 7229 of May 19, 19__ for $9922.56, you have not responded in any way. Having received no explanation for your delay, we now urgently request an immediate payment.

It is not our intention to embarrass or harass you, but we must have action on your part. If you cannot pay the invoice in full, you may write a check for half of it today.

Sincerely,

Dear Mr. Lampe:

A little over a year ago we approved a line of credit of $_____ for your company.

We have mailed you reminders, copies of invoices, and letters to notify you of your overdue account.

You have so far indicated no interest in paying, and therefore we are seriously considering terminating your credit.

Only a check within ten days for payment of all your past due invoices will keep your credit line open. The amount due is $1929.90. Why not mail your check today?

Sincerely,

APPEAL TO COURTESY

Dear Mr. Spires:

We are at a loss to understand why we have not received payment on your past due account or at least the courtesy of a reply to our several reminders.

You may have a good reason for your delay in paying, but we don't know what it is. We will try to work out an agreement for extending payments if that is what you need.

Please let us hear from you today. Your check for $302.40 would be most welcome today.

Sincerely,

Dear Mr. Penski:

Thank you for your order of August 19, 19__. We appreciate your continued confidence in our lines of quality builder's hardware.

As a courtesy to you, we will ship your order on September 3, as requested.

There is, however, the problem of a past due amount of $4412.93, about which you have received previous letters.

We hope you will respond to our faith in you by mailing a check today for the overdue amount.

Sincerely,

APPEAL TO FRIENDSHIP

Dear Mr. Dewar:

You surely understand that we cannot permit your account in the amount of $7744.55 to run indefinitely. We have tried to bring this matter to your attention in a friendly way, but such methods seem to bring no results.

We shall expect full payment within the next ten days. Your prompt attention to your past due account will be appreciated.

Sincerely,

Dear Mr. Smith:

You have been a customer of ours for nearly ten years and we consider you a personal friend.

Your account, however, has gone unpaid for too long. The overdue amount is now up to $429.75. We just can't let friendship get in the way of your paying your bill.

Could you please mail us a check today? We appreciate your business and want it to continue.

Sincerely,

APPEAL TO SYMPATHY

Dear Mr. Gordon:

We are interested in and concerned about our customers. If there is a reason why we have not received a payment from you in several months, please let us know what it is. I am sure we can be of help by extending the time for payment. By working together, we can reach a solution that is right for both of us.

Please let us hear from you. Better still, why not mail your check today?

Sincerely,

Dear Mrs. Pulver:

We too have bills to pay, and that is difficult when payments come in late.

Right now your account is 90 days past due. A check mailed today, even for half the amount, would be appreciated.

Sincerely,

_____

APPEAL TO LOYALTY

Dear Mr. Quinn:

You have been a customer of ours for over 20 years. Such loyalty cannot be pushed aside lightly. That is why we have permitted you to delay some of your payments well beyond our stated terms.

Two of our invoices are fourteen months past due. We have helped each other during many trying business slowdowns, but now we ask sincerely that you make at least a one-half payment of $_____ today.

With regards,

_____

Dear Mr. Horton:

Credit records available from our industry association reveal that your payment record with several of your suppliers is excellent.

Our experience, on the other hand, has been that you consistently have an overdue balance.

Could this be loyalty to a few preferred customers at the expense of others?

We would like to discuss this with you. Please call this week, unless of course you can mail your check today.

Your current overdue balance is $_____.

Sincerely,

_____

A PROBLEM?

Gentlemen:

We again call your attention to the following invoices which, according to our records, are still unpaid well beyond their normal terms:

Date	Invoice No.	Amount
6-17-___	1139	$1444.77
8-25-___	1289	2864.57
		$4309.34

We would greatly appreciate your informing us of the reason for your delay or receiving a payment made today.

Sincerely,

Dear Mrs. Austin:

Payment of the balance in your account was due August 31 under our open account terms. Your payment is now 60 days behind schedule.

Because our letters of September 20 and October 10 have gone unanswered, we can only assume there is no question about the amount of your balance.

We expect to receive your check for $422.55 before November 10, 19___.

Sincerely,

Re: 12/14/___   Invoice No. 84439 $1600.98

Dear Sir/Madam:

In accordance with the terms of sale on the wheel balancing equipment you recently purchased and which is now in your possession, the above invoice is due for payment.

If there is any reason for withholding payment of this invoice, please use the reverse side of this letter to explain the circumstances. If not, we would appreciate your arranging to forward settlement of this charge today.

Sincerely,

Dear Mr. Carver:

It has been 45 days since we gave you a 30-day extension on your payment. We have received neither your check nor your explanation.

We sincerely ask that you give us a reason for your delay, or, preferably, mail your check for $798.00 today. We are expecting it.

Sincerely,

Dear Mr. Lindquist:

Your July 19__ statement, copy enclosed, indicates that several items are from 30 to 90 days past due, while other more recent purchases have been paid for.

This is probably because there is a problem with some of the invoices. Please let us know what the problems are. Then we can work together to reach a mutual agreement.

Meanwhile, please mail your check to cover the undisputed items today.

Sincerely,

Dear Mr. Bushman:

Your payment of August 10, 19__ omitted our invoice No. 4-721 dated May 1, 19__ for $729.30.

We have written before about your not paying this invoice. Has it just been overlooked or is there a problem with it? If there is a problem, please discuss it with us so we can help you find a solution. If it has been overlooked, please include it in your next payment.

Sincerely,

Dear Mr. Bekins:

YOUR PAYMENT HAS NOT BEEN RECEIVED

Please send payment today or contact us at once as it must be determined what action our office should take on this account.

Payment now will clear your record.

The balance due is $1395.22.

Sincerely,

Dear Mr. Alifano:

Because cash flow has been a problem for you, as you explained in your recent letter, we have a solution for your consideration.

You reported that your inventory is in good shape, and that suggests to us that you could reduce your overdue payables balance by returning some of your inventory for credit and then paying the small remainder in cash.

Let us know if this is agreeable. If it is, we will have our salesman, Mr. Dave Hollinger, work with you to determine which items are to be returned.

We hope to hear from you in ten days with a list of items you may wish to return for credit, along with a check for the remaining balance.

Sincerely,

Dear Mr. Dusing:

As one of your sources of supply, we are often asked about your payment record. Until recently, we have had no hesitation in saying, "Pays promptly."

But what can we say now, with your account balance of $1,131.20 so far overdue? Could we work together on the problem that is delaying your payments?

Please let us hear from you this week—and we would appreciate a check to clear at least half of the overdue balance today.

Sincerely,

Dear Mr. Coco:

A review of your account reveals that your payments are made at widely spaced and often irregular intervals. That means many invoices have passed their due date before being paid.

We would like to ask your cooperation in paying invoices on a more regular basis. We suggest monthly payments within our stated terms of 1% 15 days net 30.

We appreciate your business and hope to continue serving you.

Sincerely,

Dear Mr. Baumeister:

We'll come right out and ask it. We won't guess. We won't suggest reasons you can agree to, because you are the one with the answers.

What's troubling you about the 60 pump valves you purchased on August 20, 19__?

Please let us know.

If there is nothing wrong, please mail your check today for $1587.90.

Sincerely,

EXTENDED PAYMENTS

Dear Mr. Boswell:

You have a good reason, I am sure, for not having made a payment on your account since November.

We don't know what that reason is, and we don't know how to help you unless we do.

I am confident some arrangement can be made to relieve your worry about this past due account. Perhaps an extended payment schedule would help.

Please let us hear from you. Let us help. Okay?

Sincerely,

Dear Mr. Luce:

Here we are again writing to you about your past due account. The amount is $3840.00.

We realize it may be difficult to come up with that amount all at once. We ask only that you make a partial payment of $640.00, then set yourself a schedule for continued partial payments of $450.00 weekly.

We would like your first partial payment today, please.

Sincerely,

Dear Mr. Land:

Do you agree that your outstanding balance is $972.40? We fulfilled our obligations; please fulfill yours.

If there is some reason you have not paid on time, please let us know so we can help. We may be able to arrange a longer payment term. Even better, please remit in full today.

Sincerely,

Dear Mr. Cline:

Your account is past due in the amount of $4429.57.

Installments can be arranged if you act now. In the space below, tell us what you can do. If it is reasonable, we will cooperate.

    I want to pay this account and will pay your office in installments of $_____ on the _____ of each _____ until the full amount has been paid.
Signature_____
Date_____

An envelope is enclosed for your convenience in returning a copy of this letter today.

Sincerely,

ORDERS HELD

Dear Mr. Speiling:

Your account is past due as shown here:

30 days	$475.20
60 days	329.00
90 days	400.00
120 days	299.40
	$1503.60

Unless a payment is received within ten days, we will have to hold all your orders.

Because we do wish to continue serving you, please mail your check today.

Sincerely,

Dear Mr. Falwell:

Thank you for your order of March 4.

The order is being held until we receive payment in full of your past due amount of $2498.35.

When your account is maintained on a current basis, we will be able to fill your orders as they come in.

Your current order, No. P-4371, will be shipped just as soon as we receive your check for $2498.35.

Sincerely,

Dear Mr. Elrod:

Thank you for your purchase order No. 1334 dated February 2, 19___.

We are sorry, but because your account shows a balance past due of $500.78, we must hold this purchase order until your account is paid in full.

A prompt payment will release your order.

Sincerely,

Dear Mr. Henion:

We appreciate receiving your order No. B-229-A of May 29, 19__.

Our receivables account shows you have a balance of $3339.82 that is more than 90 days past due.

When that amount is cleared, we will immediately ship your order.

We look forward to receiving your check and being of service to you in the future.

Sincerely,

Dear Mr. Richter:

Thank you for your order No. A-1127 dated October 20, 19__. It will be shipped on the date requested.

This is an exception to our policy of holding orders when a customer has a past due balance.

We feel confident that you will pay the overdue amount of $875.50 this week and pay for your current order according to our terms of 1% 30 days net 31 days.

Sincerely,

TERMS

Dear Mr. Clayton:

The attached statement shows that your balance of $1241.29 is 90 days past the due date.

You have not responded to our previous requests for payment. We cannot continue to ship to you on our 30-day open terms unless your account is brought up to date. Terms could be changed to cash-before-shipment.

To continue our current relationship and terms, please mail your check for the above amount within ten days.

Sincerely,

_____

Dear Mr. Thompson:

Recent payments of our invoices have been received long after the due date. Invoices appear to be paid in batches rather than individually when due.

Perhaps our terms are not clear, and I would like to take this opportunity to explain them.

Your credit terms are "Net 30 days," meaning that payment is due here thirty days after the date of our invoice. If you prefer to pay our invoices several at a time, we can change our terms to "15 Prox.," in which case payment is due here on the 15th of the month following the date of our invoices. However, if the total amount of these groups of invoices exceeds your credit limit, more frequent payments will be necessary.

If you have any questions about your terms, or wish to change them to "15 Prox.," please call me at 000-000-0000. I will be happy to discuss this with you.

Please remember that continued delays in paying our invoices will result in our suspending shipments to you. We presume this will not be necessary and look forward to continued business with you.

Sincerely,

_____

NO RECORD

Gentlemen:

Re: Invoice C-83301   12/13/__

During a recent audit of our accounts, we discovered that the attached invoice remains unpaid. Will you please look into this today, and if your records agree, send us a check for $499.95.

If you should find payment has been made, please give us the number and date of your check so we can properly credit your account.

Thank you,

Re: 332-CH-5118   1/3/___ $1105.51

Dear Mr. Corona:

On 4/7/___ you wrote that the above referenced invoice was paid through the Bend Bank Company on a freight payment plan. We cannot locate any record of this payment, and on 6/20/___ Mr. A. B. Wilson, manager of your Corporate Freight Audit Department, Chicago, Illinois, asked for a copy of this invoice. It was sent to his attention that day.

Now this bill still appears outstanding and we must ask that someone review the entire matter and let us know whether or not your records show that payment was made. If so, we require a check number and date in order to locate your payment and credit your account. Please forward your information directly to my attention at P. O. Box 0000, San Francisco, CA 00000.

Due to the age of this invoice, we must ask that you reply within ten days.

Sincerely,

GOOD PRODUCT

AMOUNT DUE $_____

INVOICE NUMBER_____

AMOUNT PAST DUE $_____

Dear Mr. Hall:

This is my third letter, Mr. Hall, advising you of the above situation.

Having heard nothing from you indicating any defect in our shipment or invoicing, I'm frankly concerned by your delay.

Won't you ease that anxiety by mailing your check to me? For full payment. Today.

Sincerely,

Dear Mr. Arent:

We assume you are satisfied with the boxes you purchased from us, although your account is nearly 100 days past due.

There must be a reason for your not having paid. Would you please explain your delay? It might be easier just to write a check today for $339.00.

Sincerely,

SMALL BILL

Dear Mr. Bidinger:

We fully understand why it is sometimes difficult to pay large invoiced amounts. It is hard to understand, however, why you have not paid our invoice No. 4732 of October 10, 19__ for only $25.10.

The smallness of the amount does not lessen its importance—to either of us. You have our A-22 motor, and we expect our money.

Please mail your check for $25.10 today.

Sincerely,

Dear Mrs. Winterer:

A credit person once told me that a $30.00 debt is harder to collect than one for $300.00. At that time I didn't believe he was serious. Now I do.

Your past due bill is only $28.50, but we would still like to receive what is rightfully ours. A check mailed today would be appreciated.

Sincerely,

LETTERS TO SPECIAL DEPARTMENTS

Comments

Collection letters addressed to a person or department other than the accounts payable or credit departments can have an added impact on the accounts payable section because the letter comes to them from a higher level within their own organization.

The special collection letters can be sent to the legal department, the purchasing agent, the controller, the treasurer and the president. These officers will forward the letter to the payables department.

We suggest the letters be short and to the point.

Dear ___(company attorney)___:

Several previous reminders and collection letters have been sent regarding an overdue amount of $722.10.

Could you have the proper people look at this?

Sincerely,

Dear ___(purchasing agent)___:

We have sent many letters about an overdue balance of $_____ owed by ___(your company)___.

We have nearly reached the point where future orders will be held until the past due amount is paid.

Perhaps you can help.

Sincerely,

Dear ___(controller or treasurer)___:

Monthly statements and several letters have been sent reminding your company that a past due balance remains in your account.

We must receive a check for the amount due, $583.27, or work out an acceptable payment arrangement within the next week, or we will have to restrict the amount of your credit purchases.

Sincerely,

Dear ___(president)___ :

Could you have someone look into your company's account with us, which is over 120 days past due?

Our many reminders, statements, and letters have brought no response.

The amount due is $_____.

Sincerely,

PHONE CALL FOLLOW-UP

Dear Mr. Links:

Last week, on Monday, June 4, you stated during our phone conversation that you would mail a check for $92.87 on Tuesday.

That was over a week and a half ago. We should have received your check by Thursday or Friday.

Would you please investigate and let us know where the check is?

Sincerely,

Dear Mr. Freeburn:

Confirming our phone conversation of yesterday afternoon, I am enclosing a statement of your account and a postpaid envelope for mailing your check.

We agreed that we should receive the check before June 30.

Sincerely,

CHAPTER *14*

Final Demand Collection Letters, Business to Business

The final collection letter is the last step prior to turning the account over to a collection agency or to an attorney for whatever legal action he or she thinks will open the delinquent's pocketbook.

Consumer collection agencies normally charge from one-third to one-half the amount collected. Commercial agencies may charge from one-fourth to one-third, but these and attorney fees are negotiable.

Do not mention turning the account over to a collection agency or attorney unless you follow through as stated in your letter. Failure to do this could result in litigation.

However exasperated you are, the goodwill of your debtor must be retained. Do not demean the delinquent payer or use foul language. Care is required to avoid writing anything derogatory or what the reader would consider libelous. Don't let your anger take over.

HOW TO DO IT

1. Remind the reader of the delinquency.
2. Mention past efforts to collect.
3. State the consequences of not paying now.
4. Set a specific date after which an attorney or agency will take over the collection procedure.

LAST REMINDER

FINAL DEMAND

Dear Mr. Williams:

Repeated requests for payment of $1873.92 due on your account have been ignored.

If full payment is not received in this office within ten days from the date of this letter, the account will be turned over to an attorney for collection.

If you have any questions, you may contact me at 000-0000. We urge you to mail your check today.

Sincerely,

Subject: Final Demand

Dear Mrs. Kallen:

We have had no response to our past collection efforts with regard to the past due invoices listed below:

Date	Invoice No.	Amount Past Due

TOTAL AMOUNT DUE IMMEDIATELY $_____

We request that you remit this past due balance immediately, or we will have no choice but to turn your account over for collection or litigation. We will expect your payment by _____.

Your cooperation would be appreciated.

Sincerely,

FINAL NOTICE

STATEMENT NO.   INVOICE NO.   DATE   AMOUNT

Dear Mr. Mayor:

Despite numerous reminders concerning these past due invoices, we have not received remittance or advice as to why they have not been paid.

If we do not receive payment within five days from the date of this notice, we shall:

1. Submit a report to Dun & Bradstreet.
2. Proceed with legal collection procedures.
3. Advise your customer or supplier of your overdue status.

Very truly yours,

Amount Due: $6352.08
Date Due: February 2, 19__

Dear Mr. Letterman:

You have ignored our previous requests for payment.

If payment in full is not received by the above date, the attorney representing this office will be instructed to proceed with whatever action he deems necessary. Please mail your check today.

Very truly yours,

Dear Mr. Goodrich:

We do not intend to carry your account any longer. We are instructing our attorney to bring suit if the account is not settled within ten days—by August 9, 19__. Please mail your check for $135.00 today.

Very truly yours,

Dear Mr. Haffey:

NOW is the time for action.

Your account of $873.42 is seriously overdue.

You have not responded to repeated requests for a payment on your past due account. We can no longer stand by and wait. We must have action on your part.

Unless we receive a check from you within ten days—on or before June 17—we will start legal action to make the collection. Why not avoid the extra expense and mail your check today?

Sincerely,

APPEAL TO CREDIT STANDING

Dear Mr. Prinn:

After eighteen months of numerous reminders, we find your balance of $1724.25 on our list of past due accounts.

Because we can wait no longer, our attorney will begin the necessary steps to obtain the amount owed us.

The only way to prevent this and the resulting bad credit rating is to pay this amount within 14 days from the above date. Because this is our last letter, we will allow you this two-week grace period.

We hope to receive your check within five days.

Sincerely,

Dear Mr. Gately:

We have used every reasonable means available to persuade you to pay the $2129.47 you owe us. Your refusal to cooperate makes legal action necessary.

Action by the courts becomes a matter of public record, destroying your credit standing. Court procedures are inconvenient and costly to you. You are then left to wonder why you didn't avoid all that notoriety by making an honest effort to pay an honest debt.

This is our last attempt to help you. We will allow you ten days, until August 24, 19___ to make a mutually satisfactory arrangement for payment of your debt. After that date, our attorney will proceed with court action.

Very truly yours,

Dear Mr. Kaye:

Prompt action in paying your overdue account is urged because in ten days we are required to send a list of delinquent accounts to our association's collection bureau, and we don't want your name to appear on the list.

The past due balance is $6628.50.

Please mail a payment today to keep your name off the "delinquent" list.

Sincerely,

Dear Mr. Midway:

We tried.

We are trying now.

We don't want to have to try again . . .

to collect the money you owe us. Your payments used to be prompt, but this last bill is over a year old. You have not responded to our earlier reminders, and now we must have payment by December 15, 19___.

If your account is not paid in full by then, it will be turned over to a collection agency. To avoid this inconvenience and loss of credit rating, please mail your check today in the enclosed envelope.

The amount due is $829.80.

Very truly yours,

Dear Mr. Long:

Your attention has been invited several times to our past due invoice No. 1112, but no reply or payment has been received. You have, therefore, left us with no choice but to send your account to an agency whose facilities cover your area.

We are extremely reluctant to take this step, for we know that a local record of your indebtedness and the usual proceedings that would follow might very well result in considerable embarrassment and inconvenience to you. Most certainly your credit rating would suffer.

Your remittance by mail within fifteen (15) business days from the date of this letter will stop this action. Why not mail your check today?

Sincerely,

Dear Mr. Shannon:

Our long-time efforts to convince you of the importance of paying your accounts have brought no favorable response. We have offered many varied suggestions to make your payments easier for you, but you have declined even to discuss these. The only course left to us is legal action.

This can be inconvenient and time consuming for you. It can also jeopardize your credit standing.

If you will make a payment within ten days, we will forget the legal action and consider you a paid-up customer.

We must have a one-third payment of $250.00 within ten days from the date of this letter.

Sincerely,

Dear Mr. Yates:

Our many letters about your debt remain unanswered, and the $12,725.92 balance in your account continues past due.

Therefore, we have taken steps to turn your account over to a collection agency. To forestall this action and its effect on your credit standing, please write or call us this week with your payout plans. Better yet, mail your check now.

Sincerely,

Dear Mr. Mohlder:

We have had no response from you in answer to our many phone calls and letters during the past twelve months. Our invoice No. H-2977 of June 12, 19__ in the amount of $2218.70 remains unpaid.

Our next step is to take legal action to collect the money due us. This is unpleasant for both of us and is damaging to your credit rating. However, you may avoid legal action by making payment within ten days: on or before June 10, 19__.

Whether or not we take legal action is now your decision.

Sincerely,

APPEAL TO FEAR

Dear Mr. Merkle:

You haven't made a single payment, a single reply to our letters, or a single return of our phone calls about our invoice No. 47-222 of July 1, 19__ for $22,733.34.

This invoice is now more than 120 days old, and you must agree we can no longer extend the time for payment. We are writing you this FINAL plea for payment to avoid unpleasantness.

We must let you know that unless we receive your check by November 12, 19__ we shall have to request that our attorney begin the litigation process. That can be more costly than paying your debt.

Please send your check for $22,733.34 today to avoid further action.

For your convenience, please use the enclosed, postpaid envelope.

Sincerely,

Dear Ms. Jamele:

We have written and phoned you many times about your past due balance of $_____. In all that time no satisfactory reply has been received.

It is time for us to take the next step. We <u>must</u> receive full payment within ten days, by March 23, 19__, or your account will be turned over to __(name)__, collection attorneys in __(your city)__.

Sincerely,

APPEAL TO COURTESY

Dear Mr. Mietzel:

After our many letters and phone calls in the past few weeks, we had surely expected your payment by now, or, at the very least, the courtesy of a reply.

Now, reluctantly, we must take action.

If we have not received full payment of $_____ by _____, we will refer your account to an outside agency for collection.

Sincerely,

Dear Mr. Dilley:

You made no reply to our last letter, and therefore we have sent the records of your long-overdue account balance to our attorney for collection.

There is still time for a friendly settlement.

Our attorney suggests giving you the courtesy of five more days in which to make your payment of $1002.90. If full payment or an acceptable arrangement is not received by then, he will proceed with litigation.

Sincerely,

APPEAL TO LOYALTY

Dear Mr. Nike:

Our credit department has recommended that your account be referred to our attorney for legal action. Our numerous attempts to collect from you during the past eight months have been unsuccessful, but because of our long-term relationship I am reluctant to accept that recommendation.

I will hold the credit department's suggestion in my desk for ten days in the hope that you will respond favorably by then. In fact why not mail your check for $1,825.00 today and obviate the need for further action?

Sincerely,

Dear Mr. Lehing:

Your loyalty to our company over the years is deeply appreciated. The time has come, however, when loyalty alone is not enough to keep our business going.

Your account balance has been past due for more than nine months. Our attempts during that time to have you make a payment have resulted in nothing more than, "We'll pay soon."

We can wait no longer. Preparations are underway to have your account turned over to our attorney for collection, through litigation if necessary. You now have only ten days in which to prevent this action, therefore please clear your $3,643.99 account by mailing your check today.

Sincerely,

APPEAL TO COOPERATION

Dear Mr. Hefte:

Because you have not responded to our numerous requests made during the past nine months for payment on your $1247.00 debt, we find it necessary to turn your account over to our attorney.

Perhaps your attorney could meet with ours to avoid taking this problem to court. A suit is costly, time-consuming, and detrimental to your credit standing.

You can, however, avoid the hassle of court action by making full payment by October 3, 19__. We must hear from you before then.

Very truly yours,

Dear ___(company president)___ :

Our two companies have worked amicably together for many years. Therefore you may not be aware of an overdue balance in your account of $2146.49.

We have attempted through many notices and letters to have this past due account paid, but with no success.

Your account records are being prepared for submission to our attorney for collection. We will wait, however, another ten days before proceeding further.

Sincerely,

A PROBLEM?

Dear Mr. Coulter:

It has been brought to my attention that the following freight bills remain unpaid by your company:

Freight Bill No.	Date	Amount

If there is some reason that we are not aware of that prevents you from honoring our invoices, then it is imperative that you contact us immediately.

Otherwise, I must ask you for payment in full within fifteen (15) business days from the date of this letter to avoid any outside legal collection actions.

Your cooperation would be greatly appreciated.

Sincerely,

Dear Mr. Morley:

Your current statement is enclosed and shows a past due balance of $14,398.98. All our requests to date for payment have been ignored.

Because you have not responded, we must assume that there are no questions or problems about the items listed on the statement. We must now request immediate payment.

If payment isn't received before September 20, 19___, we will turn your account over to our collection agency.

To avoid this inconvenience to you, please mail your check today, using the enclosed envelope.

Sincerely yours,

Dear Mr. Sumner:

Although a balance of $13,198.87 remains on your account, we have not received a payment since September 20, 19___. It is imperative for you to take immediate steps to settle this matter.

We will do everything we can to assist. On the other hand, if we do not hear from you, we will proceed with whatever action is necessary to recover this balance.

We expect to hear from you by February 16, 19___.

Sincerely,

Dear Mr. Raupp:

Although we have sent you a statement, three reminders, and two letters about your unpaid balance of $1719.44, we have not heard from you.

If there is a reason for not paying, please phone or write us immediately. After June 14, your account will be turned over to our legal staff for whatever action they believe appropriate. This inconvenience, however, can be avoided by mailing us your check for $1719.44 before June 14.

Sincerely,

SELF HELP

Dear Mr. Sutter:

You don't want us to call in an attorney to assist in collecting the $4429.80 you have owed us since April 15, 19___. We don't want that either.

Why not keep both of us happy by settling your account this week? A check from you on or before next Thursday will save us a call to our attorney and you the trouble of defending legal action.

Sincerely,

Dear Mr. Challis:

During the past six months, we have asked your credit and administrative officers to pay your seriously overdue account. The $4372.00 is now 180 days past due.

Our consistent yet friendly efforts have so far been in vain.

We can give you only ten more days to pay in full. If we have not received your check by August 28, 19__, we will turn the account over to our attorney for whatever legal action she finds necessary.

You can avoid this by mailing your check for $4372.00 today.

Very truly yours,

INSURANCE TERMINATION

Sitwell Service Company

Sir/Madam:

Notice of Termination of Employee Insurance Program

We have not received your monthly payment due on January 15. According to the terms of the salary deduction agreement, a payment is due and payable by the fifteenth of each month. Failure to pay during the due month is a cause for termination of the agreement. Because of non-payment the agreement is terminated upon your receipt of this notice.

Although the salary deduction agreement is terminated, the agreement will be reinstated if payments for both January and February are received by February 28. If payments are not received by then, it will be necessary for us to notify individual policy holders that they may be without insurance coverage.

If you have already mailed the payments for these two months, please disregard this notice.

Should you decide to resume your salary deduction agreement, please have your employees consult their insurance representative, who will explain the options available to them.

The total amount now due is $992.50.

If you have any questions about this notice, please phone your insurance representative at 000-0000. If not, I suggest that you mail your check today.

Sincerely,

Dear Ms. Mancuso:

Re: Policy No. 447291871-2 $4200.00

You have not responded to our many recent notices that the expiration date of your policy was approaching. Your 30-day grace period expired July 10, 19__, leaving us no alternative to canceling your policy.

You may, however, renew your coverage by writing for an application. A new policy will be issued upon receipt of your check, and coverage will begin on the date of your application. Why not renew now and mail your check today?

Sincerely,

CASH IN ADVANCE

Dear Mr. Holberg:

Because of the extreme slowness of your payments over the past two years, we can no longer extend credit to you. We have discussed this time and time again, but to no avail. Starting today, all sales will be cash-with-order.

We will be happy to continue serving you under these conditions. You can expect the same quality merchandise and the same fast service—and our super-fast emergency service.

We do expect you to make regular payments on your present balance. Appropriate collection or legal action will be taken if your failure to pay continues. Why not clean up your account and mail your check today?

Sincerely,

Dear Mr. Barz:

We appreciate your business and wish to keep you as a customer. However, because most of your payments have been late and we see no signs of an immediate improvement in your payment schedule, we must cancel your line of credit.

There will be no change in our service to you as a customer. The only change will be that we now require cash before an order can be entered.

Payments on your current balance must continue.

We look forward to an improvement in your business so we can again extend credit to you. Why not start over by mailing your check today?

Sincerely,

COOPERATION

Dear Mr. Shields:

We are sincerely disappointed not to have received any cooperation from you in answer to numerous letters asking for a payment on your account of $1,932.32 or at least an explanation of why you feel you shouldn't pay.

With a reply from you, we could have worked together on some payment arrangement. Since you don't seem to want that, we must proceed with legal action. We hope you will stop our legal steps—which you can—by making payment on or before August 17, 19__, ten days from today.

Sincerely,

Dear Mr. Cull:

Cooperation is what makes businesses run. You depend on us and we depend on you.

This doesn't seem to have worked recently. Your coopertion by paying your invoices according to our terms has been lacking to the extent that we may have to call in outside help to collect your long overdue account.

The ___(company name)___ collection agency will take over your account ten days from the date of this letter, if by then you have not paid the balance due of $4102.00.

Sincerely,

FRANKNESS

Dear Mr. Libet:

I would like to talk to you in person about your past due account. Since that is not feasible, let us talk frankly in this letter.

Your payments were on time until the beginning of this year, but since then we have received no payments. During this time you have continued to buy from us. You have ignored our past reminders. Something is wrong. Can we help? Please phone or drop in to visit so we can get together on a payment plan.

At this time we urgently request that you contact us within the next ten days. After that, we will have no choice but to cancel your credit and turn your account over to a collection agency. We don't want to do that because it may harm your credit rating. We must hear from you by November 20. The amount outstanding is $6142.29.

Very Truly Yours,

Dear Mr. Dowdle:

We feel it is in the best interest of our customers as well as ourselves to request money that is due us. We receive our money, and our customers express their loyalty, save their pride, and retain their credit standings.

We find that most of our customers respond well to fairness and to our willingness to cooperate.

When a payment is late, we mail a few friendly reminders. If that brings no response, we send out letters giving our customers an opportunity to explain the reason for not paying. We offer extended payments and delayed payments if their financial condition is uncertain.

We give our customers every reasonable chance before making the required late payer report to our _____association.

Beyond that, we sense that our customers are as willing to put up with a collection agency or litigation as to pay us.

We believe you have reached that point.

We will, however, wait another ten days before assigning your account to our attorneys for collection. After considering the consequences, you may decide to mail your check for $12,055.44 today.

Sincerely,

FIGHT FOR RIGHTS

Dear Mr. Plasky:

Do you like taking a beating without fighting back? We don't either. We don't want to fight or take a beating, but you have driven us into action.

Your bill for $541.95 is still unpaid after twelve months. We have tried all the persuasive techniques we know, and now we feel we must consider our options.

You will, however, have ten days in which to pay your bill. If we have not received the money due us by March 20, we will seek legal advice.

Please let us hear from you before March 20.

Sincerely,

Dear Mr. Hussey:

We are going to come out fighting because no other collection technique has brought results. Our straight-from-the-shoulder punch is this:

If you don't get in touch with us within ten days so we can work out an amicable method for paying your past due account, our legal department will take over your account for collection.

You know the debt is just because you have never contested it or submitted a claim against the products you received.

Litigation can be expensive as well as damaging to your reputation and your credit rating.

Our "fight" is not intended to have a "knock-out" punch, because we want your business—but also our money.

Sincerely,

_____

EXTENDED PAYMENTS

Dear Mr. Treckel:

We have expected receipt of $3148.73 for the balance due on your account for the past five months. You have not replied to our reminders and letters by either phone or mail.

We were willing to offer you an installment payment plan, but you obviously are not interested in this or other opportunities to ease your cash flow problems.

We regret that unless payment in full is received within ten days, before August 21, 19___, we will turn your account over to a collection agency.

Please send us your check today for $3148.73 so we will not have to take any action that will damage your credit rating.

Sincerely,

_____

Dear Mr. Witton:

You have not responded in any way to our recent letters about your past due account. Since February 12 you have owed us $401.00. If you do not reply by December 10, enabling us to arrange for periodic payments, our next step will be to consult our attorney about further action. We urge you to mail your check today.

Very truly yours,

_____

BUSINESS RELATIONSHIP

Dear Mr. Furth:

You have not responded at all to our attempts to collect the $991.32 you have owed us since December of 19___. This leaves us no alternative to seeking legal action.

This step requires unnecessary time and trouble for both of us. Therefore, we will delay any action for ten days from the date of this letter. If we receive your payment by then, we will be happy to continue our business relationship.

Please mail your check for $991.32 by January 22.

Sincerely yours,

Dear Mr. Carlson:

It is difficult to write an old friend a letter that may not end up being considered friendly.

That is because of the several invoices (copies attached) that have been past due for many months.

We have sent numerous reminders and letters requesting payment or an explanation for not paying, and we have offered methods of paying in easy installments.

We are very patient with old friends, but we also have to consider our own financial responsibilities.

Therefore, following a grace period of 15 days, your overdue invoices will be sent to our attorney for the necessary collection procedures. Please consider the consequences and mail your check today.

Sincerely,

DAMAGED GOODS

Dear Mr. Copeland:

We notified you several weeks ago that it was noted on the bill of lading that there was considerable damage to the merchandise you crated and transported for us.

If we are not informed within ten days of the date of this letter how you wish to dispose of this damage claim, we will turn this matter over to an attorney for disposition.

I trust your answer will be favorable.

Sincerely,

Dear Mr. Mould:

We have notified you previously of damage to seven desks you moved to our Norwood plant on March 29, 19__, our bill of lading No. A-77295. We have filed a carrier claim with you and sent two reminders of our claim.

To date we have received no reply.

If no response is received within 15 days from the date of this letter, the claim will be turned over to our attorneys.

Sincerely,

Dear Mr. Mack:

You have failed to respond to my previous letters concerning the damaged stoves received on your BL No. A-772976 dated July 24, 19__. It now becomes urgent that we hear from you no later than _____. Otherwise, we will have no alternative except to pursue other action to resolve this dispute.

You may call me directly at 000-000-0000.

Sincerely,

Dear Mr. Tait:

In spite of your lack of response to our many letters about our billing for repairing the typewriters shipped to us on March 24 and received April 30, we still believe that there must be a reason why you have not paid us. Unless we know your problem, we cannot help you solve it. You agreed that we would make the repairs and bill you.

We are asking for a reply within 15 days, by October 16, 19__, because, with no reply, after that date your account will be given to our collection agency for whatever action they deem necessary.

Please contact us before October 16. We can work together on a satisfactory payment plan.

Sincerely,

BROKEN PROMISE

Dear Mr. Kahn:

The balance due Marmon Company of $9928.00 is now due and payable. Your inability to live up to your commitments and frequent misrepresentation of information is very disheartening. Therefore, I will set a deadline of June 30, 19___ for receipt of the entire balance.

If the balance is not received by that date, I will request the assistance of a local collection agency or hire counsel for the resolution of this matter. Please be aware that Marmon Company reports credit experience to credit gathering agencies.

Sincerely,

Dear Mr. Mathieu:

You have failed to keep your commitment given to me to pay $_____ by _____ toward the reduction of your past due account.

Unless you pay your committed amount by _____, I will have no alternative except to pursue other action to collect from you.

If you have any questions, please contact me at 000-0000.

Sincerely,

Dear Ms. Whitehead:

As of this date, our invoice No. 4-3189 dated March 12, 19___ in the amount of $1200.50 is open on your account.

I have contacted you numerous times in an attempt to work with you in resolving your balance. Each time I called I was given a date by which payment would be made. None of these promised dates were kept.

Because your account has been overdue for so long, it is imperative that payment be made immediately. If payment in full, $1200.50, is not received in my office within ten days from the date of this letter, I will begin other actions to collect the money due.

I urge you, Ms. Whitehead, to give this matter your immediate attention.

Sincerely,

NEGLECT

Dear Mr. Spaulding:

We have reminded you many times of your $_____ past due account.

You have yet to offer even partial payment or a response of any kind.

We simply cannot understand your neglect of this serious matter.

Accordingly, we now advise that unless we receive full payment by _____, we will refer the matter to our attorneys.

Do let us have your payment and save us both this extra time, effort and expense.

Sincerely,

Dear Mr. Finch:

Your neglect of your seriously past due account in the amount of $_____ has now obliged us to take measures to protect our interests.

You have been granted ample time to pay this account. Consequently, we have scheduled the claim to be placed with local counsel representing our company if arrangements are not made to pay your overdue amount by _____.

This notice gives you a final chance to settle directly with us.

We trust that you will take advantage of the extension. You may call me personally at 000-000-0000.

Sincerely,

Dear Mr. Tembe:

Your apparent disregard of your seriously past due account, now amounting to $994.32, has required us to take steps to protect our receivables.

We have reminded you many times that payment is due. Now we have scheduled the placement of a claim with a collection agency if payment in full is not received by __date__.

This is a FINAL notice. Your dealings after __(date)__ will be with the collection agency or their attorney.

We request that you take advantage of this grace period to make payment directly to us

Very truly yours,

SKIP TRACING

Comments

A good place to start locating a "skipped" customer is on his credit application. Persons and businesses mentioned there can be contacted. Writing letters to people who might know of the debtor's whereabouts is just one of many locating techniques.

Dear Ms. Spartan:

You were given as a reference by John T. Tilden when he applied for credit. He has now moved, and we have no forwarding address.

We would appreciate your writing his current address at the bottom of this letter and mailing it in the enclosed envelope.

Sincerely,

Dear Mr. Williams:

We are attempting to trace Ms. Joan Bette Arndt. We understand she was recently employed by you. Could you give us her present residence or business address?

Do you know of someone who could give us this information if she left no forwarding address with you?

Your help will be appreciated.

Sincerely,

CHAPTER 15

Series of Collection Letters, Business to Business

Often a delinquent customer or borrower needs only a reminder that the last payment was not made. Because of this, many firms use a series of from three to six short collection letters. These can be form letters typed each time as originals, or they can be pre-printed—even in booklet form—with spaces for filling in the amount and due date. Each letter is more insistent than the previous one. When these will suffice, the time and cost required for composing personal letters can be saved.

The time interval between letters in a series will depend upon business conditions, how much you need to cater to the particular customer, and your cash flow situation.

Alternate your sets of series occasionally and develop a routine for mailing them.

Use the shortest series you find effective, because if your customer <u>knows</u> you will mail six collection letters, he or she will wait for the sixth before paying.

Normally, four letters should collect your money. If they don't, special attention-getting techniques can be used. Colored envelopes and paper make <u>your</u> letter stand out from the ordinary white. Use pink, buff, green, orange, yellow, red, or others. Also, unusual transmission techniques will draw attention to your letter. Overnight letters, registered letters, express mail, telegrams, and telexes are effective changes from the common place. **Bold print**, CAPITALS, <u>double underlining</u> and unusual lettering styles also attract attention.

HOW TO DO IT

1. Let the reader know this is a collection letter.
2. Mention one or more facts related to the particular situation.
3. Request prompt payment.

SERIES ONE, THREE LETTERS: PAST DUE INVOICE

Letter One

Dear Mr. Tooly:

Enclosed is our invoice No. G-2971 in the amount of $199.80 for your order of May 21, 19__ and the bill of lading for shipment on May 22, 19__.

Terms are net 30 days.

Please mail your check to P. O. Box 0000, Sacramento, CA 00000.

Today, please.

Sincerely,

Letter Two

Dear Mr. Tooly:

Your June 19__ statement is enclosed. Please note that $199.80 is 15 days past the 30-day due date.

We must request immediate payment of this past due item.

If there is a question about the amount, please send us an explanation so we can clear your account.

A postpaid envelope is enclosed for your convenience. Please mail your check today.

Sincerely,

Letter Three

Dear Mr. Tooly:

Re: Invoice No.   G-2971
      Invoice Date   May 22, 19___
      Balance Due $199.80

This is the last request we will make directly to you to pay the invoice shown here.

If no payment is received by September 29, 19___, we shall take whatever steps are necessary to collect the $199.80 due us. Why not mail your check today?

Sincerely,

SERIES TWO, THREE LETTERS: PAST DUE BUSINESS ACCOUNT

Letter One

Dear Mr. Neal:

According to our records, your current balance is $510.51. Of this amount, $250.41 is more than 30 days past due. As you know, our normal terms require payment within 30 days after the invoice is sent to you.

Since you have established an excellent credit rating with us in the past, we are surprised to see a problem arise at this time. If there is some error, or you are unable to pay the amount due immediately, please contact me so that we can correct the situation or make suitable arrangements for prompt payment of this balance.

If all is in order, please mail your check today. Your attention to this request is appreciated.

Sincerely,

Letter Two

Dear Mr. Neal:

We have not received any response from our statements of the last two months or to our letter of September 15. Your entire account is now 45 days overdue, and you owe us a total of $510.51.

If there is some reason why this payment cannot be made immediately, please contact us so we can make arrangements that will be mutually agreeable. Perhaps we can work out a payment schedule that would be realistic for your present circumstances.

Naturally, we do not want to endanger your credit rating or destroy the good relationship that we have maintained in the past. Therefore, would you please take care of this overdue balance immediately?

We have enclosed a postage paid envelope for your convenience. Please return it with your check for $510.51 today.

Sincerely,

Letter Three

Dear Mr. Neal:

We still have had no response from our statements of the past three months or from the letters we sent you on September 15 and October 15.

Your entire account is now seriously past due. It is obvious that our efforts to clear the account on a mutually agreeable basis have had no impact.

Unless we receive payment from you within ten days or can work out a mutually agreeable arrangement for payment, we will have to report your delinquency to the Retail Credit Bureau.

Following that, the account will be turned over to our attorneys for further action. Since this is a costly procedure for both of us, and will damage your credit rating, I would suggest you call immediately, or mail your check for $510.51 today, so we can clear your account without resorting to such procedures.

Very truly yours,

_____

SERIES THREE, THREE LETTERS: PAST DUE FREIGHT BILL

Letter One

_____

Gentlemen:

Attached are copies of our freight bills that are past due. Just a reminder that we require payment within ten days.

We would appreciate prompt payment.

Sincerely,

_____

Letter Two

_____

Gentlemen:

Although we sent you past due reminder copies of the attached bills three weeks after our original billing date and again after five weeks, the charges remain unpaid and are now seriously past due.

Since we know you wish to pay your bills when due, we expect that these open items are just an oversight on your part.

Our published tariff prohibits us from extending credit to customers who have past due charges outstanding, and we therefore have no alternative but to withdraw credit privileges in such instances.

We would very much like to continue extending you credit, and you will enable us to do so by mailing your remittance today.

Sincerely,

Letter Three

Gentlemen:

Two weeks ago we wrote to you with copies of the enclosed freight bill numbers advising you that they were seriously past due and in violation of our credit policy.

We assumed that failure to pay these open items was an oversight on your part and that our letter would bring a prompt response and enable us to continue extending credit. We regret to see that they are still unpaid, and the past due status of your account leaves us no alternative but to remove your company from our list of credit customers. Our terminal manager has been instructed to rescind your credit privilege and transact future business on a cash basis only.

If the outstanding balance is not paid within ten days, our Collection Department will take whatever action is necessary to accomplish collection.

Sincerely,

SERIES FOUR, THREE LETTERS: PAST DUE SEASONAL PURCHASE

Letter One

Dear Mr. Newquist:

Has preparation for the arriving early-summer painting season kept you so busy you have forgotten our last invoice for paint and supplies? Our invoice No. 29144 for $2429.81 is thirty days overdue.

Please pay this invoice today so your account will be clear when you're ready to order again. We expect second orders to be heavy this season, and we are prepared to fill rush orders from our paid-up customers. We're counting on you to be among them, so please mail your check today.

Sincerely,

Letter Two

Dear Mr. Newquist:

We have not received payment of our invoice No. 29144 for $2429.81 that we reminded you of in our letter of March 4, 19__. We are concerned because you are now forty-five days overdue.

Late payments do not look good on your credit record, and, as we indicated in our first letter, paid-up customers receive preferential treatment.

If extended payments would be of help to you, please contact us, and we can work out some arrangement that will be satisfactory to us both.

Please use the enclosed envelope to mail your check today.

Sincerely,

Letter Three

Dear Mr. Newquist:

Payment of our invoice for $2429.81 is 123 days past due today.

You have not responded to our offer to extend your payments. In fairness to our pay-on-time customers, we cannot carry your account any longer.

Turning your account over to our attorney for collection can only damage your credit standing further.

This unpleasant alternative can be avoided by your paying the full amount of our invoice by June 17, 19__—ten days from today.

Sincerely,

SERIES FIVE, THREE LETTERS: TERMS OF SALE

Letter One

Dear Mr. Ainsworth:

Our records show that the following purchases by you are past due:

May 29, 19__	$761.30
May 30, 19__	292.00
June 4, 19__	476.10
	$1529.40

It is to your advantage as well as ours to keep your credit account current.

We would appreciate your paying these amounts today.

Sincerely,

Letter Two

Dear Mr. Ainsworth:

You did not answer our first reminder of your overdue balance of $1529.40. Could you have overlooked our terms of 1% ten days net thirty days? If there is a reason for the delay, please let us know. Otherwise, prompt payment today would be appreciated.

Sincerely,

Letter Three

Dear Mr. Ainsworth:

Once again, Mr. Ainsworth, we ask for your cooperation in paying your past due account.

A prompt receipt of $1529.40 will keep your account open so we can be of help when you make future purchases.

Since we don't want to have to take any further action, we will expect a check dated today.

Sincerely,

SERIES SIX, THREE LETTERS: CREDIT REPUTATION

Letter One

Dear Mr. Vessey:

Your account balance of $222.14 is now twenty days past due.

May we have your payment soon? Today?

Sincerely,

Letter Two

Dear Mr. Vessey:

Again we suggest payment of your overdue balance of $222.14.

Your delay in taking care of this balance is harmful to your ability to get additional credit with us and with other suppliers and is destroying your reputation as a desireable customer.

You can overcome these business obstacles by paying your account today. Please take advantage of this opportunity by mailing your check today.

Sincerely,

Letter Three

Dear Mr. Vessey:

We can no longer continue to carry your account. We believe you realize that we are in effect financing your business when you do not pay your bills on time.

Here is our FINAL offer to help you: You may pay the $222.14 owed us by December 14, 19___. If payment is not received by then, our attorney will contact you to arrange means for settlement.

Sincerely,

SERIES SEVEN, FOUR LETTERS: NEW START

Letter One

Dear Mr. James:

Would you make your payment of $9103.00 by the end of this year?

Starting out the new year with a current account should make it a pleasant and successful one.

An envelope is enclosed for your convenience.

Sincerely,

Letter Two

Dear Mr. James:

Your account is overdue. Your prospering firm has a good reputation. We feel that it is important that you keep your account up to date in order to maintain this reputation. Please pay today. The amount due is $9103.00.

Sincerely,

Letter Three

Dear Mr. James:

The balance of $9103.00 is now six months beyond our sales agreement. There has been no response to our last two letters. We are expecting this payment from you within the next five working days.

Sincerely,

Letter Four

Dear Mr. James:

You have not paid the balance of $9103.00 on your account that is now nine months overdue.

If this amount is not paid by the last day of this month, we will place it with a collection agency. This action will damage your credit rating.

Sincerely,

SERIES EIGHT, FOUR LETTERS: REPUTATION

Letter One

Dear Mr. Rice:

We hope that this year has been a pleasant and successful one for you, and that next year will be even better.

To end this year happily, we would like to see you clear your past due balance of $392.10. A check mailed to us today will start your new year with a current balance.

An envelope is enclosed for your convenience.

Sincerely,

Letter Two

Dear Mr. Rice:

A good reputation is essential to a prospering business, I am sure we both agree.

Your past due account, however, does not seem to support your good reputation. We feel it is important for you to get your account on a current basis. Please mail your check today. The amount is $392.10.

Sincerely,

Letter Three

Dear Mr. Rice:

Your account is nearly six months beyond our terms of net thirty days. I am sure it is not your intention to ignore past due notices at the expense of your credit rating.

We strongly suggest that you make a payment within the next four days.

We are expecting you to mail your check today for $392.10.

Sincerely,

Letter Four

Dear Mr. Rice:

The balance of $392.10 in your account does not warrant any more of our time and expense to collect. We also feel it should not be placed with a collection agency.

We can write it off as a bad debt, but your credit reputation will suffer. Uncollected accounts are reported to our trade association. Your credit standing can be maintained, however, by a prompt payment made no later than the end of this week.

Sincerely,

SERIES NINE, FOUR LETTERS: TERMS OF SALE

Letter One

Dear Mr. Gurtner:

A review of our records indicates that you have an overdue balance of $611.00. Our terms, as you know, are 1% 30 days net 31 days.

When may we expect payment? Why not mail your check today?

Sincerely,

Letter Two

Dear Mr. Gurtner:

A second reminder of your past due balance of $611.00 seems necessary. Our terms are clear that payment is required on the 31st day following your purchase.

May we have your check for $611.00? Please mail it today.

Sincerely,

Letter Three

Dear Mr. Gurtner:

Past due accounts concern us. Your balance of $611.00 is now 60 days beyond our terms.

We appreciate that many reasons may account for your delay. Our standard terms of 1% 30 days net 31 days are adequate for most of our customers. In unusual cases, however, these terms can be extended to overcome temporary difficulties or to accommodate unusually large purchases.

Please tell us your reason for not paying on time. We can perhaps extend your payments or suggest other ways to refinance your operations.

The amount due is $611.00. Please contact us or mail your check today.

Sincerely,

Letter Four

Dear Mr. Gurtner:

Our offers to help you in reducing your overdue account have gone unheaded. We have been patient for six months, but can no longer let your balance ride along.

Regretfully, this is a final notice.

We will receive your check for $611.00 in ten working days, before October 21, 19___, or your account will be turned over to our attorney for collection.

Very truly yours,

SERIES OF FIVE OR SIX LETTERS

Comments

Only on special occasions should you plan to use a series of more than five or six letters. These occasions would be when there is a personal relationship between the creditor and the debtor.

It is also wise to vary the number of letters in the different series you mail to any one customer. When your customer becomes aware of a pattern of six letters, he or she may decide to wait for number six before approving your bill for payment.

SERIES TEN, FIVE LETTERS: EXPLAIN DELAY

Letter One

Dear Ms. Edwards:

No doubt you have overlooked payment of the enclosed statement. Your prompt remittance would be appreciated.

Account No.   _____

Date Due   _____

Payment Due $_____

Sincerely,

Letter Two

Dear Ms. Edwards:

Your attention is again directed to your past due account. To avoid an unfavorable report of your credit records, we suggest immediate payment of the amount due.

Account No.   _____

Date Due   _____

Payment Due $_____

Sincerely,

Letter Three

Dear Ms. Edwards:

It is apparent that you have ignored our two previous reminders. Your account is now past due.

We request that you pay this account immediately or personally discuss it with us.

Account No.   _____

Date Due   _____

Payment Due $_____

Very sincerely yours,

Letter Four

Dear Ms. Edwards:

There must be a reason for not paying your account. Whatever the reason, we would be happy to discuss it with you. We can make arrangements for smaller payments over a longer period of time if that would help you. We must hear from you or receive a check within the next fifteen days.

Account No.   _____

Date Due   _____

Payment Due $_____

Sincerely yours,

Letter Five

Dear Ms. Edwards:

Since you have apparently made no effort to pay the amount due us, we have no alternative to taking legal action. You may prevent this, however, my making payment by August 15, 19__.

Account No.   _____

Date Due   _____

Payment Due $_____

Very truly yours,

SERIES ELEVEN, FIVE LETTERS: EXTENDED TERMS

Letter One

Dear Mrs. Denney:

We sincerely hope you have no objection to a reminder that there is a balance of $999.52 on your monthly account.

If you haven't mailed your check, could you do it now? Then your account will be current.

Cordially,

Letter Two

Dear Mrs. Denney:

You did not respond to our first reminder of your overdue account, but we have confidence that you will mail us a check for $999.52 to make your account current.

Please use the enclosed postage paid envelope to mail your check today.

Sincerely,

Letter Three

Dear Mrs. Denney:

We are interested in our customers and are always looking for ways to improve our customer service. For this reason, we would like to know if there is a reason for your delay in paying your long-overdue account. If there is some way we can help—by making your payments smaller, by extending our terms, or by recommending a loan company—please let us know today.

We would appreciate a word from you—or preferably a check for $999.52.

Sincerely,

Letter Four

Dear Mrs. Denney:

Several times by letter and phone we have discussed arrangements for the payment of your account. The following items are still past due:

No. 1527	5-4-___	$229.70
No. 1574	6-4-___	320.00
No. 1622	6-7-___	449.82
		$999.52

So far we have received no indication of your cooperation. Thus at this time we request an immediate payment. Please use the enclosed postpaid envelope to mail your check today.

Sincerely,

Letter Five

Dear Mrs. Denney:

Is there anything we can do to persuade you to pay your seriously overdue account? We have tried many friendly suggestions for extending the payment period, for making small monthly payments, for seeking help from lenders, and for at least discussing this matter with us.

We can't give up, but we have about exhausted our own resources. Therefore, we propose to seek aid from outside our own company. Our attorney has been consulted, and he reports that various legal avenues are available for collecting our money.

We dislike even the thought of going to court, and have decided to extend your credit for two weeks—only fourteen days. To avoid legal action, we must have your check for $999.52 on or before August 16.

Sincerely,

SERIES TWELVE, FIVE LETTERS: COOPERATION

Letter One

Dear Mr. Foster:

Did you forget the last invoice we sent you? It is easy to do, we know. Perhaps all you need is a short reminder that the amount is $303.20 for the three socket wrench sets you purchased. A check mailed today would be appreciated.

Sincerely,

Letter Two

Dear Mr. Foster:

May we again remind you of the invoice we mailed you in February for $303.20?

It will be more convenient for both of us if no more reminders are required. Please mail your check today.

Sincerely,

Letter Three

Dear Mr. Foster:

We have not heard from you about our February invoice for $303.20 for three socket wrench sets. Your account is now 35 days past due.

It is easy to misplace an invoice or to put off payment, we realize. Please delay no more. We ask that you mail your check today.

Sincerely,

Letter Four

Dear Mr. Foster:

Our last three letters regarding your past due account of $303.20 have not been answered. We anticipated full payment or partial payment or at least an explanation for not paying.

If there is some difficulty with the wrenches or your ability to pay now, please let us know. We can work with you to make your payments easier, but we must know your problem before we can help you solve it.

Please let us hear from you today.

Sincerely,

Letter Five

Dear Mr. Foster:

Your February 19___ invoice for $303.20 remains unpaid.

Your complete lack of cooperation has us puzzled. You have made no apparent effort to make a payment or to give us your reasons for not paying.

Needless to say, your credit standing has suffered.

We will give you one last opportunity, however, to redeem your credit rating and your reputation. We must receive your check for $303.20 by September 30, 19___, or we will turn the collection task over to the Caldwell Collection Agency.

Very truly yours,

SERIES THIRTEEN, SIX LETTERS: SLOW PAY BUSINESS ACCOUNT

Letter One

Dear Mr. Andres:

Why not start right now to check these invoices that are past due?

No. 14112	5-4-__	$ 229.80
No. 15627	6-4-__	3320.00
No. 15811	6-8-__	429.82
		$3979.62

By paying them now, you save the trouble of having to check them again. If there is a reason for their not being paid, please let us know. If all is in order, please mail your check today.

Sincerely,

Letter Two

Dear Mr. Andres:

If at first you don't succeed . . .

Here is your second opportunity to pay these past due invoices:

No. 14112	5-4-__	$ 229.80
No. 15627	6-4-__	3320.00
No. 15811	6-8-__	429.82
		$3979.62

We know you intend to pay them, so why delay? If you have reason for not paying, please mail us an explanation or phone us at 000-0000. Otherwise please mail your check today.

Sincerely,

Letter Three

Dear Mr. Andres:

This is our third letter. May we ask:

Why haven't you paid?

Why haven't you written?

Why haven't you phoned?

Do you intend to ignore your bills?

Surely not, so please mail your check today for $3979.62, covering invoices 14112, 15627 and 15811.

Sincerely,

Letter Four

Dear Mr. Andres:

With reluctance but apparent necessity we remind you once more of your open account that is now 60 days beyond our 30-day terms.

Our previous reminders have apparently been ignored, but you can no longer delay payment if you wish to keep your account open.

Please call us now to discuss ways we can work together to reduce your open balance. We will do what we can to help you.

Don't fail us and your company at this time. At the very least send us an explanation for your delay. A check sent today will keep your account open.

Sincerely,

Letter Five

Dear Mr. Andres:

Any further delay in paying your balance due cannot be accepted. Your apparent desire to reject our suggestions of working together on getting your account current is having a bad effect on your credit record. We must have a payment at once.

If you cannot send at least a partial payment right now, call us so we can arrive at some workable agreement.

Please respond today.

Sincerely,

Letter Six

Dear Mr. Andres:

Ten days, ten short days, is the amount of time our legal department suggests we extend your open account. After that time—July 26—our legal staff will take action to collect your overdue account.

This decision should not seem blunt or surprising. We have repeatedly written and phoned your office asking for payment. Your response has been negative. We can no longer be sympathetic. You can surely understand why we must have your cooperation.

To avoid further action, please mail your check for $3979.62 on or before July 26.

Sincerely,

SERIES FOURTEEN, SIX LETTERS: COOPERATION REQUESTED

Letter One

Dear Mr. Corwin:

We all appreciate an occasional reminder of a forgotten invoice. Perhaps you mislaid this one of March 13, 19__ for $1307.00. We are enclosing a copy.

Won't you write a check and mail it in the enclosed envelope—today, please?

Sincerely,

Letter Two

Dear Mr. Corwin:

We are enclosing another statement of your balance of $1307.00.

Since this amount has remained long past our thirty-day terms, we feel an immediate payment should be considered by you. Please mail your check today.

Sincerely,

Letter Three

Dear Mr. Corwin:

Your account balance of $1307.00 is still unpaid.

Not having heard a word from you, we assume you do not question the amount you owe us.

Now we ask that you pay without delay. Please mail your check today.

Sincerely,

_____

Letter Four

_____

Dear Mr. Corwin:

You received monthly statements from us for March, April, May, and June. You received phone calls from us on April 14, May 15, and June 12. You received letters from us dated April 29, May 30, and June 30.

The results: negative responses.

It is our policy to help our customers as much as possible because we appreciate their business. If you have a problem with our merchandise or with your finances, please let us know what it is so we can help. But we must hear from you to understand what the problem is.

Please phone or write today. That will help us both.

Sincerely,

_____

Letter Five

_____

Dear Mr. Corwin:

Should we take drastic action to collect the balance you owe us? Is drastic action necessary?

We hope not. But our letters have been unanswered and our phone calls ignored. A payment by you can no longer be put off. Please send at least a one-fourth payment with a word of explanation about future payments toward your account of $1307.00.

We must have your cooperation if we are to work with you in getting your account on a current basis.

Action is required NOW. Please mail your check today.

Sincerely,

Letter Six

Dear Mr. Corwin:

Your balance of $1307.00 remains unpaid in spite of our continuous and friendly reminders asking for payment or an explanation for your delay.

It seems that our only recourse now is to take strong measures to collect from you. We will, however, be patient for another ten days. If full payment is not received by August 31, 19__, we will pursue legal action.

We hope to receive your reply in three days.

Sincerely,

SERIES FIFTEEN, SIX LETTERS: FUTURE CREDIT LIMITED

Letter One

Dear Ms. Ingalls:

Our records show the following amounts now due:

Current	$249.80
30 days	121.10
60 days	375.42
	$746.32

Please mail your check today to cover these amounts. If payment has already been mailed, you may disregard this letter.

Sincerely,

SERIES SIXTEEN, SIX LETTERS: CREDIT STANDING JEOPARDIZED

Letter One

Dear Mr. Nielsen:

Your check for our December 28, 19___ invoice, No. 43211 in the amount of $529.80, has not been received by our office.

If it has been mailed, thank you. If not, please consider this just a reminder to mail your check today.

With regards,

Letter Two

Dear Mr. Nielsen:

Our December 28, 19___ invoice for $529.80 is still unpaid. If you did mail your check, please let us know the date and your check number so we can review our records.

Otherwise, please mail your check today.

With regards,

Letter Three

Dear Mr. Nielsen:

You have not acknowledged our previous two letters about our December 19___ invoice for $529.80. It is now 45 days past due.

Your credit rating is in jeopardy. To maintain your credit standing, please mail your check before you put this letter aside—today, please.

With regards,

Letter Four

Dear Mr. Nielsen:

We are disturbed when we still see your $529.80 balance on our accounts receivable computer printout.

When you ordered the electric motors from us, you expected prompt shipment, and you received prompt shipment. At the same time, we expected prompt payment but have not received any payment or even an explanation for your not paying.

Your credit rating can be restored, but only by mailing your check TODAY.

Regards,

Letter Five

Dear Mr. Nielsen:

Let us be frank and strictly "business." You purchased electric motors from us in December of 19__. Your cost was $529.80. That was _____ days prior to the date of this letter.

Your response has been zero. You have made no payments and you have not provided us with an explanation for delaying your payments.

What we can do is to allow you seven days from the date of this letter to make payment in full. On the eighth day, if we have not received your check, we will turn your account over to our attorney for whatever action he finds necessary to collect from you.

Regards,

Letter Six

Dear Mr. Nielsen:

The final limit we gave you for paying your $529.80 bill has passed. We feel our only method of collecting is to obtain outside help.

Any further correspondence or communication you receive about this overdue amount will be from our attorney. He will contact you soon. Why not avoid the additional expense by paying before he sues? Mail your check TODAY.

Very truly yours,

COLLECTION AGENCY COMMERCIAL LETTERS

Letter One

John's Nursery, Inc.

$447.90

Dear Mr. Glaspell:

Your account, as shown above, has been turned over to us for collection. It is not my desire to work a hardship on you, but I must insist that this account be settled within ten days from this date.

Please contact me so we can make arrangements to take care of this balance.

Sincerely,

Letter Two

Dear Mr. Cleary:

Re: Baskins Supplies

   Amount Due: $2437.46

On June 28, 19__ the above account was turned over to me for collection, and at that time I wrote you asking that you make immediate settlement. Since I heard nothing from you, I advised you that I was referring the account to an attorney and instructing the attorney to start suit.

Four days after sending you that notice, Mr. Rogers of __(creditor's company)__ phoned and asked that I delay any action because he thought you would settle. He notified me today, however, that you had paid nothing on this account and requested that I go ahead with the action.

I am writing you today to give you another opportunity to make settlement in full or a partial payment or to make some arrangement for handling this account. I must hear from you by January 12, or it will be necessary for me to proceed with creditor's instructions to refer the account to an attorney for suit.

Sincerely,

Letter Three

Dear Mr. Cohansey:

This notice is sent to you by Collection and Adjustment Bureau, a collection agency.

Date ....March 14, 19__

In Re...FC No. 73004215

Creditor ....Boling Merchandisers

Debtor...............................Mr. Richard B. Cohansey

Address..........................000 Wash Street, City, State

To avoid errors, please make all payments payable to and mail them directly to this office.

Enclose a check or money order and mail immediately in the envelope provided.

AMOUNT DUE

Principal...$214.42

Interest 14.64

Court Costs...54.00

Total Due...283.06

IF PAID NOW

Sincerely,

Index